LEVEL 1

GIRLS THAT ARE STRONG, SMART AND PURE

LEVEL 1

GIRLS THAT ARE STRONG, SMART AND PURE

Nihil Obstat
Reverend John Balluff, STD
Censor Deputatus
April 29, 2016

Permission to Publish
Most Reverend Joseph Siegel, DD, STL
Vicar General
Diocese of Joliet
May 2, 2016

ISBN 978-1-5051-0936-8

Published in the United States by
Saint Benedict Press
PO Box 410487
Charlotte, NC 28241
www.SaintBenedictPress.com

Printed in the United States of America

Contents

LoveEd: An Introduction for Parents

It's no secret that today's culture is confused about love and sex. Movies, television, the Internet, and music expose children at an early age to twisted perceptions of romance and relationships. In a culture that is morally adrift, parents need the right tools to help them navigate their children safely through the dangerous temptations and distorted perceptions of sexuality.

As you attend the *LoveEd* event and work through the rest of this book with your child at home, both of you will discover the amazing truth that human sexuality has a wonderful meaning and purpose. That vocational purpose is passed on from generation to generation for those who love God and seek to serve Him, and is fulfilled when a man and a woman create a new family on their wedding day. In this family circle, children will learn how to love God, others, and themselves. *LoveEd* will help parents guide their children through the circles of love: *God's love, family love, friendship love, and an understanding of a future romantic love.*

Through the experience of this program, and along with their parents' help, children will learn that:

- God has made them to be a loving human person, both body and soul.
- God has planned for them to go through physical changes called puberty.
- God has called them to be strong, smart, and pure throughout their lives.
- God has created them to receive His love and share this amazing and pure love with others.

Level 1 of the *LoveEd* program will discuss the physical changes that occur during puberty and how these begin to prepare children for married life. It will also explain the male and female powers to co-create life with God. Level 2 will explain how a child is created through God's natural and supernatural plan, and how a baby grows in the mother's womb from conception to birth. The Parent Training Event and accompanying *Parent Guide* provide you with additional information to assist you in communicating these sacred messages to your child and answering other related questions that may arise over time.

However, it is not enough for children to know about bodily functions. Human beings are much more than biological cells and systems—we are persons made in God's image! Working through *LoveEd* will give you the tools you need to teach, from a Christ-centered perspective, about some of the important changes that will be going on in your children's bodies during the next few years, as well as the vital connection puberty has with their vocation to love and the development of virtues. When virtues are practiced, especially chastity, it can lead your children to a life of self-giving love and truly prepare them for adulthood.

Your children have the right and responsibility to know information about their growth, which is both biological and spiritual. God's special plan for sexuality is best discussed in a personal conversation with you in the context of sound Church teaching. Attending this event and reading this book will help you and your children start the conversations that will help them understand themselves and their place in God's plan.

LoveEd can be the beginning, or the continuation, of those ongoing conversations with your children about life, love, and purity, conversations that can extend into their adulthood. It's important, now more than ever, for you to guide them while they develop a holy awe of God's amazing creation of life!

PART I

Parent/Child Event

Complete the following six Acts by watching each video and answering the discussion questions with your Mom.

ACT 1

The Story of You

Introduction

The first Act introduces us to a fifth grade girl named Mariana Garcia, as well as her family and friends. We will see her in her daily life as she handles some of the struggles that come with growing older.

 Watch Act 1

Mother and Daughter Discussion

Read these questions and answer them with your Mom.

1. How is the Garcia family like your family?
   - ☐ They all live in the same house.
   - ☐ The kids have chores to do.
   - ☐ There are little kids in the family.
   - ☐ They eat together at the dinner table.
   - ☐ Other similar things include: _____ .

2. How is the Garcia family different from yours?
   - ☐ Their parents are married, and mine are not.
   - ☐ They live in the suburbs, but I do not.
   - ☐ I am the oldest, and Mariana is not.
   - ☐ They are not allowed to sleep late, while I am.
   - ☐ Other differences include: _____.

3. What did you like about Mariana?
   - ☐ She was cute.
   - ☐ She liked to have silly fun.
   - ☐ She obeyed her parents.
   - ☐ nothing
   - ☐ everything, including: _____

4. What did Mariana do that was good?
   - ☐ She was kind to Sarah.
   - ☐ She made her little sister laugh.
   - ☐ She helped in the kitchen.
   - ☐ other _____

5. Did you like Sarah?
   - ☐ Yes, because she seemed like a fun friend.
   - ☐ No, because she tried to get Mariana to watch bad movies.
   - ☐ No, because she liked boys and ignored her friend.
   - ☐ Yes, because she could do whatever she wanted.

6. Ask your Mom to tell you about a friendship she had when she was young that drifted apart when they became interested in different things.

7. Tell your Mom if something like that has happened to you when a friend started acting differently, and ask her what she would do about it. Do you have any friends who act differently around boys?

8. What are two things you could do or say if your friend wanted to watch a show or look at a website that you knew your parents didn't want you to watch? Ask your Mom to add one more thing after you have told her your ideas.

(1)

_____

_____

_____

(2)

_____

_____

_____

Mom's Idea

_____

_____

_____

In anticipation of viewing the Act 2 video, please complete the following activity.

At the center of the circle named "Family," write the names of the people in your immediate family and/or those who live in your home. On the outside edge of that circle, write the names of other close family members, such as grand-parents and close cousins or relatives you see often and love very much.

At the center of the circle named "Friends," write the names of your closest or favorite friends. On the outside edge of that circle, write the names of other kids you hang around with.

In the next Act, we'll learn what the third dotted circle is and why you are not yet within it, but might be one day in the future.

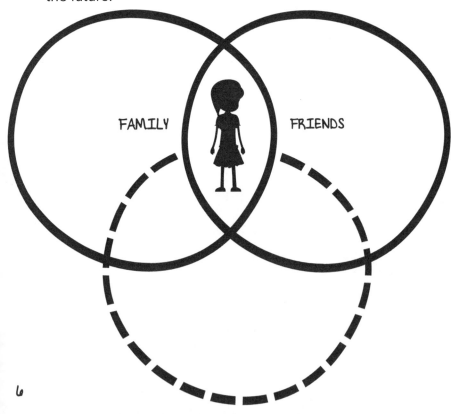

Affirming the Good

Ask your Mom to tell you about a time she was proud of you. Have her write it down so you can read it later.

ACT 2

Growing in Circles, Growing in Love

Introduction

The second Act has some important things to tell you about the three circles in our diagram and about God's plan for you and your life.

 Watch Act 2

Mother and Daughter Discussion

For this section, refer to the list of virtues as you go through and answer the questions. The column on the left lists some of the virtues that you are developing in your family love circle. The column on the right shows some of the virtues needed to build good friendships. The middle column represents the virtues needed for you to be who God created YOU to be.

The word "virtue" here is meant to encompass "character strengths." These words describe the many areas of human goodness.

Love Requires Virtue

FAMILY VIRTUES	PERSONAL VIRTUES	FRIENDSHIP VIRTUES
Respect	Faith	Cooperation
Sharing	Modesty	Humility
Obedience	Good Judgment	Leadership
Caring	Integrity	Fairness
Patience	Compassion	Independence
Forgiveness	Confidence	Trust
Gratitude	Courage	Confidence
Helpfulness	Self-Denial	Honesty
Responsibility	Chastity	Courtesy
Truthfulness	Competence	Teamwork
Kindness	Initiative	Goodness
Courage	Thoughtfulness	Self-Control

1. Ask your Mom to pick three of the virtues in the Family column that she sees you practicing on a daily basis. Have her put a plus sign (+) next to those three and explain why she is picking them.

2. Now, you pick three virtues from the Family column that you know you need to work on more. Mark them with a minus sign (-) and tell your Mom when and how you will try to practice those more often.

3. Next, think about the kids you spend most of your time with. Pick three of them and write down their names. Beside their names, pick one of the virtues from the Friendship column that they practice often. Tell your Mom about a specific time each friend practiced that virtue.

Friend: _____ Virtue: _____

Friend: _____ Virtue: _____

Friend: _____ Virtue: _____

4. Ask your Mom to pick three virtues either from the Family column or the Friendship column that she wants you to practice when you're with your friends. Have her tell you some examples of how you can practice them.

Virtue _____

Virtue _____

Virtue _____

5. The Personal Virtues in the center list have to do with you and your efforts to be the unique individual God created you to be. Write down three and tell your Mom the meaning of them and how you can practice them. Then have your Mom pick three more and give her own examples of how you can practice those.

Personal Virtues I want to work on:

Virtue _____

Virtue _____

Virtue _____

Personal Virtues Mom suggests that I work on:

Virtue _____

Virtue _____

Virtue _____

6. The video told us that the virtues are like spiritual muscles we have to exercise every day if we want to be morally strong. We also have to exercise our physical muscles.

If you are doing this event in a group, wait until the Facilitator tells you all to do this at the same time.

See how many jumping jacks (or sit-ups) you can do in one minute. Ask your Mom to keep count.

I can do _____ jumping jacks (or sit-ups) in one minute.

ACT 3

God's Story . . .
From the Beginning

Introduction

Act 3 zooms out to God's view of the universe and helps us learn that everything we are and everything we have is a gift of God's creative love. Watch carefully in the video for some pictures of Bible stories that show God's love.

 Watch Act 3

Mother and Daughter Discussion

Listed below are some quotes from the video. Take turns reading them with your Mom and discuss the questions.

1. "God made the whole world, and He made it amazing." Name some of the things in God's world that you think are amazing.

_____

_____

_____

2. "God made fish to swim, animals to run, and planets to circle the sun." What did He make us human beings to do?

_____

_____

_____

3. "God gives every human being two great gifts that make us capable of loving–the ability to know and understand (intellect) and the power to make free choices (free will)." In what ways do human beings misuse these gifts?

_____

_____

_____

4. "Sin is a choice to turn away from God. Sinful choices tear families apart, ruin friendships, and corrupt romantic relationships." Discuss some of the unloving choices that can cause these bad consequences.

_____

_____

_____

5. "When we are children, our parents try to protect us from all harmful things." What are some of the ways your parents have tried to protect you from evil? Ask your Mom to help you think of these ways, and have her explain why she and your Dad did these things.

_____

_____

_____

6. With your Mom's help, draw lines to match the Bible story with the lesson of God's love that it teaches us. Ask her to talk to you about how each story applies to family life today. If you need help, search for the following passages: Luke 15:11-32, Luke 24, John 19, Luke 10:25-37.

The Prodigal Son	Jesus Christ took the punishment for our sins because He loves us so much.
The resurrection of Jesus	God is a loving Father, and He waits with open arms to forgive us when we are sorry for our sins.
The crucifixion of Jesus	When we are wounded by someone else's sin, God sends someone to bring us the healing power of His love.
The Good Samaritan	God's love is stronger than sin and death. He redeemed us with His great love.

7. Tell your Mom about a recent time you remember seeing love being shared within your family. Ask her to also tell you about a loving family time that she remembers. Write down a few words to describe those times, which will help you recall them later.

_____

_____

_____

8. The video ends by saying: "Now it our turn to help create a loving world." Name some of the ways you and your family are trying to do this.

_____

_____

_____

Affirming the Good

Mom, you can see that I love God when I

_____

_____

_____

_____

_____

Mom, I can see that you love God when you

_____

_____

_____

_____

_____

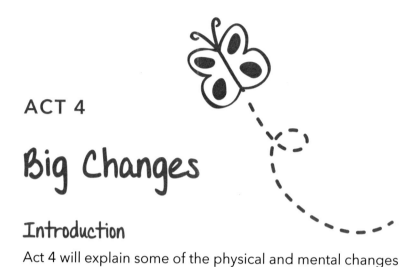

ACT 4

Big Changes

Introduction

Act 4 will explain some of the physical and mental changes that occur in your body during the years of puberty.

➡ Watch Act 4

Mother and Daughter Discussion

1. Review the female anatomy diagram on the next page with your Mom and answer these questions. This will help you understand what's going on inside your body. Use the following answer key: A. Uterus or womb, B. vagina, C. y, D. ovary, *One of these letters is used twice.*

   The _____ releases an egg cell once a month.

   The _____ is also called the birth canal.

   The _____ is the tunnel through which the egg cell travels.

Female
Anatomy
Diagram

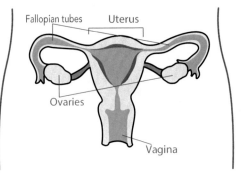

The _____ holds the menstrual blood until the end of the month.

The _____ surrounds the baby when a mom is pregnant.

2. Check off the goals below once you accomplish them.
   ☐ I know the proper names of my body parts.
   ☐ I can refer to the proper names if necessary without laughing or being embarrassed.
   ☐ I know that God created women's breasts to make milk for a baby after it is born.
   ☐ I understand the purpose and the basic workings of the menstrual cycle.
   ☐ I know how to respond with virtue when I feel moody.
   ☐ I have some ideas of how to use my extra energy to do good for myself and others.

3. Changes are already taking place in your body. Check all that apply and talk to your Mom about them.
   ☐ I need to use deodorant.
   ☐ I need to wear a bra.

☐ I'm getting hair in new places.
☐ It is more difficult to control my moods.
☐ I get tired more often.
☐ My hips are getting wider.
☐ I got my first period.
☐ I am getting taller.
☐ I am getting smarter.
☐ Other changes I want to tell/ask Mom about.

4. It's important to manage your emotions as you mature. Pick at least three emotions that you have experienced recently and draw lines to a virtue that could help you manage it. Explain your choices to your Mom and ask her for help if you need to.

EMOTION	VIRTUE
Anger	Confidence
Confusion	Courage
Excitement	Forgiveness
Fear	Humility
Indecisiveness	Joy
Irritability	Kindness
Jealousy	Obedience
Nervousness	Peace
Sadness	Patience
Stubbornness	Trust

5. You will want to be a virtuous person as you grow from a girl to a woman. Ask your Mom to name a virtuous role model you can follow. Write down some of the good qualities that person has.

_____

_____

_____

Affirming the Good

Mom, you see me growing into a woman when I:

_____

_____

_____

Mom, you help me understand what it means to be a woman when you:

_____

_____

_____

ACT 5

The Journey towards Love

Introduction

Act 5 helps you learn how to live God's love as a teenager and adult. You will learn some tips on how to become *strong* in your decisions, *smart* in your knowledge of life, and *pure* in your thoughts and actions. Listen for the good news that there are many people who are here to help you along this journey.

 Watch Act 5

Mother and Daughter Discussion

The main goal of the *LoveEd* program is to help *you* become *smart*, *strong*, and *pure* as you move toward womanhood. The next activity will help you review with your Mom how much you have learned.

Understanding Life and Love (with my Intellect)

In order to be *smart* about your womanhood, you need to understand many things about life and love. Some of these are listed below. Read each item to your Mom and mark it with one of the following signs:

✝ A plus sign means you understand it and accept how important it is. You can use two or three plus signs if you find it especially important. Tell your Mom why.

? A question mark means something about it is still not clear to you.

☐ God created me for love. As I walk the path of life, God wants me to *learn* to love and to *choose* to love.

☐ The most important "school" where I am learning how to love is my own family.

☐ When I truly love someone, I choose what is best for the other person instead of always thinking of what I want for myself.

☐ It is important for me to choose friends who can help me to practice virtue and become my best self.

☐ I am learning to love in my family and my friendship circles by practicing virtues every day—virtues like respect, patience, gratitude, responsibility, forgiveness, honesty, and cooperation.

☐ The changes in my body that begin at puberty are God's way of preparing me to be a wife and mother someday.

☐ As I move through adolescence, God wants me to develop true friendships with many girls and boys, getting to know them as persons and respecting them as friends.

☐ Someday, when I experience romantic relationships, the virtue of chastity will help me to be pure, to be friendly and kind to the young men I date, and to expect them to treat me with respect.

☐ Marriage is a solemn vow to God by which a man and a woman promise to love and care for one another until death and create a loving family together.

☐ God wants my life to be a *gift of love* either to my future husband and family, to God and the service of the Church, or in generous service to the world as a single person.

Making One Good Choice after Another (with my Free Will)

In order to be spiritually *strong* and *pure*, you need to practice virtue. You acquire virtues by making one good choice after another. Listed below are some *good choices* that will help you become a responsible and loving adult. You can make these choices, with the helping grace of God, as you follow His plan for you to choose real love.

Read each item to your Mom and mark it with one of the following signs:

✝ A plus sign means you understand it and accept how important it is. You can use two or three plus signs if you find it especially important. Tell your Mom why.

〜 A question mark means something about it is still not ˅ou.

.t my parents and help them to make my .ace where people love and respect one

☐ I will ask for—and listen to—my parents' guidance concerning friendships, entertainment, the Internet, and sexuality.

☐ I will choose friends who have positive values and can help me to live up to the virtues my family has taught me.

☐ I will be a good and trusted friend. I will stand up for kids who are being picked on or bullied.

☐ I will be friendly and respectful to boys—talking with them, getting to know them, and doing class assignments and projects with them.

☐ I will avoid using alcohol and drugs—anything that will weaken or destroy my ability to make good choices.

☐ I will dress and act modestly, avoiding clothing and activities that could draw attention to my body rather than to my interests, talents, and values.

☐ I will pray every day for the grace to be a loving person in my family and friendship circles and to make good choices that will help me to be morally strong.

☐ I will go to Mass every week and really participate in the prayers and singing.

☐ I will try to remember that Jesus walks with me every minute, always encouraging me to be the best, most loving person I can be.

Now walk through this map with your Mom and review the meaning of each little icon.

Map From the Journey towards Love Video

List one message that struck you as powerful as you watched Act 5:

_____

_____

_____

Affirming the Good

1. Mom, you see that I am being spiritually strong when I

_____

_____

_____

2. Mom, you see that I am being smart about my
   womanhood when I

_____

_____

_____

3. Mom, you see that I am committed to being pure when I

_____

_____

_____

Finish by telling your Mom when she most helps you
become strong, smart, and pure.

_____

_____

_____

Planning Time to be with my Mom

Before you begin the final Act, fill in the following with each other to make a commitment with your Mom to work together on Part II of the program. You will be reading each chapter and answering the discussion questions with your Mom.

Mom, let's plan *now* when we will finish Part II of this *LoveEd* program at home.

The best day of the week for us to spend time alone together is _____.

The best time of day for us to spend time alone together is _____.

The best place for us to spend time alone together is _____.

Let's plan to do . . .

Chapter 1 on _____ at _____ o'clock

Chapter 2 on _____ at _____ o'clock.

Chapter 3 on _____ at _____ o'clock.

Chapter 4 on _____ at _____ o'clock.

Chapter 5 on _____ at _____ o'clock.

Chapter 6 on _____ at _____ o'clock.

Thanks, Mom!

To complete Part II of the program, you will need to read each chapter before meeting with your Mom.

ACT 6

Prayer and Blessing Ceremony

This final Act in *LoveEd* leads us back to God our Father who loves us. By now we all know that we need God's grace in order to love well. Jesus, as a young adolescent, was determined to follow God's will.

In lieu of a video for Act 6, with mothers and daughters together, read and discuss the Bible story of Jesus with His parents in the temple at age twelve (Lk 2:41-52). Focus on the last part of the passage that says Jesus was "obedient" to his parents and that he "advanced in wisdom and age and favor before God and man."

Discuss why it is important to always obey your parents, as well as God the Father, in order to grow in wisdom and in grace.

Once your discussion is complete, each mother and daughter will read a prayer of blessing for each other.

A Parent's Blessing

God, our Father and Creator,
You have entrusted to me the life of [name]
as a gift from You.
She is a gift to our family and to the world.
Thank You for her.

As [name] moves through her adolescent years,
may she continue to grow, as young Jesus did,
in wisdom, strength, and grace.

Beloved God, guide her each day
as she makes her life a gift of love,
to You and to all people.
Help [name] be strong, smart, and pure,
full of faith, hope and love.

God, I ask Your blessing on my dear daughter.
Pour out Your grace on her and draw her close to You.
Through Christ our Lord.
Amen.

A Daughter's Prayer for Her Mother

God, our Father and Creator,
I thank You for my Mom.
Bless her with Your great love and mercy.
Help her to be the best mother she can be:
a woman of virtue and strength.
Give her the courage and faith she needs to
teach me and guide me
so that we both may do Your will and create
a more loving world.
Amen.

PART II

At-Home Follow-Up

Once you get home from the Event, work through these six chapters. They will help you review the information found in the videos and provide more ideas about educating yourself for real love. Answer the questions after each chapter and discuss your answers with your Mom so she can help you discover practical ways to live these lessons.

CHAPTER 1

Changing Me, Changing Friends

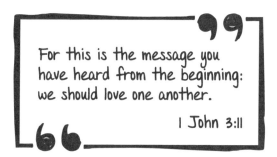

For this is the message you have heard from the beginning: we should love one another.

1 John 3:11

Celebrate life! You are a bright young girl getting ready for a fabulous adventure–the exciting journey towards womanhood! Over the next few years, you will grow from being a girl to a preteen . . . from a preteen to a teenager . . . and from a teenager to being a young woman. During this journey, you will go through a stage of life called puberty. This is a natural process when your body will begin to change from being a little girl's body to a grown woman's body.

Between the ages of ten and twelve, you are considered a preteen. During this time, your mind may be racing with new and different thoughts. Your emotions might be bouncing around like a ping-pong ball, and your body is slowly beginning to be transformed into a woman. Sometimes you may even secretly wish you could just remain a little girl. This is a time when many things will be changing in your life, but the changes are good. Why? Because God has planned these wonderful changes to happen for a reason; God has planned for every girl to grow up to be a woman and to serve Him with her life's choices.

No matter which vocation you choose—whether married, single, or religious—God wants you to grow into a beautiful young woman who is healthy and happy. He wants you to grow physically, mentally, emotionally, and spiritually. He wants you to be strong, smart, and pure. Along the way, as you grow, you will need the support of your family, friends, and the Church. And, along the way, as you read this book, you will have another friend by your side—someone who will walk with you and share with you her own trek from girlhood to womanhood. Introducing . . .

Mariana's Story

Like you, Mariana is a preteen. She enjoys playing with her friends, telling funny jokes, tickling her baby sister, Bella, and sharing a room with her older sister, Julia. They live with their mother and father, Mr. and Mrs. Garcia. Today, Mariana is planning for her eleventh birthday party! Let's take a sneak peek . . .

Sitting at her bedroom desk by an open window, Mariana chewed the end of her pencil and tapped her feet. She was thinking about whether or not to invite her friend Sarah to her party. Mariana smiled as she remembered the summer before. She and Sarah spent almost every day together, filling and throwing water balloons at each other during the hottest days. On the Fourth of July, their parents purchased sparklers for them. In the warm night air, they jumped around and waved the crackling, bright, colorful sparklers until they burned out. Once, Mariana and Sarah were sitting together in the kitchen eating fresh-baked cookies and drinking milk. Mariana took a mouthful of her milk, and, mid-gulp, Sarah made a funny face at her. Mariana burst out laughing so hard that she spit her milk out everywhere—even through her nose! Sarah screamed with hilarious joy. "With Sarah, I have so much fun," thought Mariana.

Then she frowned, remembering how Sarah had gone to another school in the fall. Being at different schools meant they couldn't see each other as much anymore. Sarah had changed a lot in just one year. "I've tried to still be her friend," thought Mariana, "but she has other friends. Besides, all she wants to do now is talk about those boys at her school." When Sarah wasn't talking about boys, she was watching TV shows that Mariana's parents would never allow her to watch.

One evening at Sarah's house, she had asked Mariana, "Do you always do everything your parents tell you to do?"

Mariana had been so shocked; she didn't know how to answer at first. Then she said, "Well, I don't always like my family's rules. But I know that my family loves me. They give me rules because they want the best for me."

Sarah snorted and chuckled before turning back to the TV program she had been watching. Mariana left Sarah's house that day feeling very sad.

After Mariana got over the memory of that feeling, she thought about her decision again. She had to decide whom to invite to her birthday party. She looked at the invitation she was creating for Sarah. Should she throw it away? Should she give up on their friendship?

Feeling frustrated, Mariana crumpled the paper and tossed it into the wastebasket. Mariana looked at the dresser where she had pinned a photo of her and Sarah. It was a picture of them laughing together, their arms locked just before jumping from the dock into the cool lake waters. Mariana sighed. "Things used to be so easy," she thought. "Now life seems more complicated. Everything seems to be changing—especially my friend, Sarah."

Mariana couldn't decide what to do. Should she walk away from her friendship with Sarah or reach out to her and try to have some wholesome fun again?

Suddenly, Mariana remembered her mother's wise advice: *Real friends never give up on each other.* Then she remembered something else her mom told her. "As you spend more time with friends, you have to make sure your friends live by our family's same values."

"I don't know what to do," Mariana thought. "This is what Mom probably meant when she said I have to learn to make more grown-up decisions."

Mariana thought about her mother's words, and then she thought again about Sarah. She thought about all the years they had fun together. And then she said to herself, "I think I will invite Sarah to my party. She needs to have some fun just as much as I do. After all, we have celebrated our birthdays together for five years."

Mariana reached down and grabbed the crumpled invitation. "I'm not ready to give up on Sarah, yet," she said aloud. Smoothing out the invitation, she began to write, "Sarah, you are invited to my Eleventh Birthday Party!"

Celebrate God's Plan

In God's big, wide, and beautiful world, there is a special time for everything that happens.

There is an appointed time for everything, and a time for every affair under the heavens.

Ecclesiastes 3:1

The seasons change in ways that we expect. When the tree leaves begin to fade to orange and yellow, you know that fall has come. Then the leaves begin to fall to the ground and we know that winter is on our doorstep. Your mom turns the heater on in the house, and your mom makes hot cocoa. If you live in the north, you probably sled down long hills or ice skate on the pond. If you live in the south, you enjoy a colder breeze and more rain.

But then winter gives way to spring. The snow melts, and the ground grows green with tender grass. You put away your heavy coat and warm sweaters and start wearing your cooler blouses and shorts. When spring blooms into summer, we go to the beach and lather on the suntan lotion.

God has planned a predictable cycle of seasons. We can depend on the predictable changes we see in the world around us. Each event—from day to night, fall to winter—happens at a time that we expect.

Did you know that God has a special design for people, too? God has planned for all of us to grow and change. After all, nobody stays a child forever—even your mom and grandmother were once tiny babies. Each person, according to God's plan, is born as either a male or female baby. God created these two specific kinds of people—*male and female*—because each one reflects Him in a unique way. Being a girl is something you can be proud to be. God made you that way.

Just like seasons change, you are on the adventure of growing and changing from a girl to a woman. No matter where you are in the adventure of growing up, one thing never changes about you, and that is your gender. You may be called a baby at one stage and a preteen at another stage, but no matter what stage you're in, one thing is certain: You started with a female body, and you will always have a female body. This science of life was written in your body when God created you in your mother's womb.

Celebrate the Changing You

Although your gender never changes, your role in life does. First you were a baby, then you became a girl, and now you are about to enter a new stage in life. You are becoming a preteen! This is the time when you will experience puberty. Puberty is a natural part of life. It is something that God planned for you. In fact, your body is already preparing for puberty. God programmed natural chemicals in your body to start working during puberty.

These natural chemicals are called hormones. All people have hormones in their bodies at every stage of their lives. These hormones are produced and sent out by your endocrine and reproductive systems. Hormones send signals to various organs of the body telling them to grow and change. God also designed your body with automatic control centers called glands. The pituitary gland in the brain sends signals through your bloodstream to tell your body to grow. When you are a child, the pituitary gland sends growth hormones into your bloodstream. Those hormones tell your bones, muscles, and other tissues to grow. When you're a preteen, the pituitary gland tells your body to begin changing from a girl to a woman. We will talk more about the biological and physical changes of puberty in chapter 4.

Celebrate Being Strong

What does it mean to be strong? Does it mean being able to lift a car like Superman? Of course not! Lifting two thousand pounds of steel is impressive, but there's more to being strong than having amazing muscles. Strength is the ability to make right choices for your body and soul. Your soul includes your mind and your will, and it is also affected by your emotions. When you choose to act in good and healthy ways that pleases God, you are being strong! When you make good choices for your body and soul, you become happier.

God wants you to be strong in your talents and gifts. God is the giver of all gifts. He is the source of your talents, abilities, and personality. Whether you're writing a poem or baking cookies, you are glorifying God. You glorify God when you say, "Thank you for making me just the way that I am! I am determined to be the best 'me' I can be."

Each girl is unique by God's design. God made each person in the world with different talents, special hobbies, and distinctive personalities. Whether you play the piano, the flute, or the guitar, whether you like to sit and plant flowers, run up hills, or go fishing, God wants you to express all the special gifts and talents He's given to you. You may have a knack for making people laugh, or perhaps you're one of the lead singers in your school choir. Maybe you enjoy painting and are pretty good at it, or maybe you are a good listener. No matter what you do, when you share your talents and gifts with others, you are giving glory to God. As you grow from being a girl to a preteen, you can become strong physically, mentally, and emotionally. You can learn to make powerful and good choices.

Being Strong Physically

Sports, exercise, and doing hard work can help your body get stronger. A sturdy body can lift, carry, run, push, and jump. Girls and women can work hard to make their bodies strong at any age. Some girls enjoy taking walks, and others like riding bikes. Even doing chores around the house can help a girl's body get strong. Girls can build their muscles through raking leaves, playing volleyball, carrying the little children they babysit, or by mopping the kitchen floor.

Not all girls can do all things, however. Sometimes people are born with bodies that don't work perfectly. Sometimes illness or injury can change our bodies. Yet it is still possible to build a stronger body, even if your body can't do all of the things you would like it to. Maybe you know somebody like Mariana's friend Lilly, who has asthma. Lilly cannot run because running makes her lungs hurt. So Lilly makes her body stronger by taking walks. Perhaps you know someone like Mariana's cousin Justine, who cannot use her right hand. Justine has learned to write, sew, and eat her food with her left hand. Being strong means making good choices with your body and learning to rise above your limitations.

Being Strong Emotionally

During your preteen years, as you begin the journey called puberty, it's normal for you to feel many kinds of emotions. You may feel excited one minute and sad the next, or you might experience frustration more often and want to lash out at others in anger. Feeling angry or "blue" can drag you down if you let it.

God wants you to make good choices about your feelings. You can be strong emotionally and learn to control your moods so they don't make you want to hurt yourself or others. When you experience a powerful emotion such as sadness or jealousy, you do *not* have to act on it. Instead, you can choose to *think* before you act. Ask yourself, "Why do I feel like this? And what should I do about it?" Maybe you're angry with someone you love, and you need to forgive that person. Maybe somebody has hurt your feelings, and you need to talk to your mom or grandmother about what to do in order to forgive them. Before you act on any emotion, think first. You can learn to manage your feelings in many new and grown-up ways. Remember that you're not a two-year-old anymore! You're a young preteen girl. Remind yourself that you will *feel*, then *think*, and then *act!* And most importantly, while you're thinking, *pray* about what God really wants you to do.

Being Strong Mentally

As you begin the journey of puberty, you will notice that you're thinking new and interesting thoughts. You begin to understand bigger and more important ideas. It might be a new understanding of your math, history, or literature. Maybe you're more creative or more interested in people of different cultures and understanding why they do what they do. You might start thinking more about what you will do when you grow up. You might daydream so much that your mom has to ask you the same question over and over before you hear her!

So, as your body begins to slowly change, expect your mind to grow, too. You'll get smarter, and you may have more questions in your mind. After all, adults need to think big thoughts and know many things in order to live a grown-up life. It's important that you look for the right role models who can help you grow in your understanding, and it's important to find good people who can help you answer your questions.

Growing Up to Make Good Decisions

A small child starts to obey because they are told to or because they want to please their parents. Now that you're older, you need to make those good decisions part of yourself. You need to grow to *want* to do what is right, not just because you *have* to. Wanting to do what is right is a good sign that you're growing up.

Sometimes making right choices means making a sacrifice. It isn't easy, but it's God's will that all Christians show the world our love for Him by obeying His commandments. The Ten Commandments are the basis for our moral decisions. They help us know right from wrong and how to treat others and respect God. It's important to understand all ten of the commandments so that you can learn to make moral decisions on your own. Do you know the Ten Commandments? If not, this a good time to memorize God's most important laws from the Old Testament. To help you get strong mentally, it's a good idea to review them each night and ask yourself questions to see how well you followed them each day.

An Examination of Conscience for Preteens Using the Ten Commandments

1. I am the Lord your God. You shall not have strange gods before Me.

Do I study my faith regularly to learn more about God? Do I pray each day and think of God often? Do I love God with my whole heart and try to grow in love for Him?

2. You shall not take the name of the Lord your God in vain.

Do I use God's name carelessly? Do I say any bad words

when I am angry? Do I show respect for religious words, ideas, and people?

3. **_Remember to keep holy the Lord's Day._**

Have I tried to get a ride to church for Mass if I needed one? Do I discuss the priest's homily with my family on the way home from church? Do I show God's love to others in an extra way on Sundays? Do I take time to study the Bible, _Catechism,_ or saints on Sundays?

4. **_Honor your father and your mother._**

Do I obey my parents? Have I done my chores without complaining? Have I been disrespectful to my parents or teachers or coaches?

5. **_You shall not kill._**

Do I keep my patience, or do I lose my temper? Do I hold grudges and try to get even with others? Have I been mean to someone because they were different? Do I criticize others and kill their spirit or their joy?

6. **_You shall not commit adultery._**

Have I failed to show respect for the bodies of others as well as my own? Do I avoid TV shows or music that treat people's bodies disrespectfully?

7. **_You shall not steal._**

Have I taken something that belongs to someone else? Have I "forgotten" to return something that I borrowed? Do I play fairly? Do I ever cheat at school or games? Have I copied someone else's homework?

8. **_You shall not bear false witness against your neighbor._**

Have I been honest, truthful, and fair, or have I lied?

Have I gossiped and talked about someone else behind his or her back? Have I said anything bad about another person, even if it was true?

9. *You shall not covet your neighbor's wife.*

Have I looked at immodest pictures rather than looking away from them? Have I been jealous of someone else's friends? Have I dressed in an immodest way or tried to show off my body?

10. *You shall not covet your neighbor's goods.*

Have I been jealous of the things my friends have? Have I nagged my parents into buying things because my friends have them? Have I helped others when they needed help? Have I given to the poor?

If you haven't already done so, this is a good time to memorize the Ten Commandments for life. This is your covenant with God; it shows Him you are on His team. You should try to follow them as your basic laws each day of your life.

Wrap It Up

In God's big, wide, and beautiful world, there is a special time for everything that happens. It's time for you to take that journey to womanhood—to grow up to be a fine young woman who knows, loves, and serves God. Be glad to be a girl, and be glad to be you! Now, make it your goal to be the best YOU that you can be.

Being a girl is something you can be proud to be! There are special gifts that come with being a girl that boys don't have. Being a female is a biological and physical reality. Your body has been programmed by God to be a female from the start to the finish! God wants you to grow into a beautiful young woman who is healthy and happy. He wants you to grow physically, mentally, emotionally, and spiritually. He wants you to be strong, smart, and pure.

Let's begin this journey to womanhood with great joy and anticipation, knowing that we will be following God through this great adventure of life.

Discussion Questions

Answer and discuss these questions with your Mom.

1. When was your last birthday party? How did you decide whom to invite?

_____

_____

_____

2. Do you have friends who act differently around boys? Why do you think this is so?

_____

_____

_____

3. What would you do if your friend wanted to watch something that offended God's plan for love?

_____

_____

_____

4. List your family's top three rules. How do these rules help everyone in the family?

_____

_____

_____

5. Which chores do you do regularly at home? Which ones could or should you do better?

_____

_____

_____

6. Can you recite all Ten Commandments in order? Keep practicing until you can.

Chapter Reflections

While discussing this chapter, my Mom gave me some extra advice about . . .

_____

_____

_____

While reading this chapter, I learned these two important things:

1. _____

2. _____

I resolve to live out the *LoveEd* teachings from this chapter by . . .

_____

_____

_____

Finish this chapter with the following prayer:

Dear God, I have heard that You love me, and I know that I love You, too. As I grow up, I hope to learn even more what this means. I know that You love me more than I understand now. And I want to love You the best that I can. Thank You for my family and my friends and the love they show me. Thank You for loving me since before I was born and loving me forever. Amen.

My Mom and I completed this chapter on

_____

(date and time)

CHAPTER 2

God Expects (and Helps) Me to Grow in Love

> Love is patient, love is kind. It is not jealous, [love] is not pompous, it is not inflated, it is not rude, it does not seek its own interests, it is not quick-tempered, it does not brood over injury, it does not rejoice over wrongdoing but rejoices with the truth. It bears all things, believes all things, hopes all things, endures all things.
>
> 1 Corinthians 13:4–7

God made no other person just like you. You are one of a kind. He made only one person who looks exactly like you, thinks exactly like you, and has the exact talents you have. God looked at the whole world and the whole plan of history and He saw one thing missing—you—and so He filled in that gap.

God wanted someone with your color hair, your height, your size, your freckles, your contagious laugh. Maybe He wanted someone with your ability to look at problems and fix them, or He wanted someone who was smart but not a show-off. In Mariana's case, maybe God was looking to create someone who was happy and outgoing and made other people feel good. He probably wanted someone as loyal to her friends as she was.

Mariana made a thoughtful decision to support her friend even though she had very mixed feelings about Sarah's changing behavior. Mariana made up her mind to give Sarah another chance. She took a big step out of her kids shoes into grown-up ones by making a difficult choice.

God gave each person the ability to make choices for themselves. This is called free will. Free will is the ability to choose where you want to go and who you want to be and how you want to act. You can live for yourself, or you can live to give glory to God. This is shown by the choices you make every day.

If we made choices based just on how we were feeling at the moment, do you think all those choices would be good ones? Probably not. So, in addition to free will, God gave you your intellect—the ability to know things. You don't merely follow instincts like a cat or a dog. You don't shine like the sun. You don't see things like a bird. You *know* things. You can figure out what is true and what is not true. You can figure out what is good and what is not good. You can laugh at yourself when you are being silly. You can appreciate what is beautiful and remember it and tell someone else about it. God gave you this gift of an intellect to carry His dignity as a human being, and He gave you your free will to help you make good choices.

Why Did God Create You?

You know the answer: God created you to know Him with your mind, love Him with your whole heart, serve Him with all your talents, and be happy with Him forever. God has a plan for teaching you to love and for helping you to become the unique and special person He created you to be. But what, really, is love?

Love is sacrificing yourself and your own wants and needs for the good of those around you and giving your time and talents in service to God and others.

God's plan for learning love can be represented by three circles: the family circle, the friendship circle, and the romance circle. Since before you were born, you've been growing inside the circle of your family. Your mother and father are in this circle, as well as your brothers and sisters and all of your extended family members (grandparents and cousins and aunts and uncles).

But as a preteen, you're entering the new circle of friendship. This circle includes all the boys and girls in your neighborhood, school, and church. When you become a woman, you may choose the vocation of marriage. If you do, you will enter the circle of romantic love. It is an extraordinary place where a man and a woman begin their journey toward marriage.

All three circles reside in the center of one beautiful, giant circle: *the circle of God's love*. This sphere wraps around all of the other circles. The circle of God's love is bigger than the universe, more glorious than the snowy mountaintops, and deeper than any ocean. Like the air you breathe, God's love flows invisibly between the circles of family, friendship, and romance. God's love helps you—and everyone else in the circles—grow closer to each other and to Him.

You are there in the center of God's three circles. You are full of God's love, which He placed inside you at your baptism. You are to share God's love with others and learn more about God's love in each of these three circles. His love moves in, through, around, and to you, your family, friends, church, and all of creation.

Celebrate the Family Circle

God created the earth, with its majestic mountains and roaring seas. He planted fruit-bearing trees and fragrant flowers. He created buffalos, turtles, and parrots. He made freshwater springs and rich soil that can produce the tasty foods we like to eat. He gave us everything on earth that we need to grow strong bodies. He also gave us something that helps grow our souls. God gave us families. It is in the circle of our families that we first learn about God and His great love for us. Within the family, we learn how to give and receive love.

Besides your parents, brothers, and sisters, the family love circle includes your grandparents, aunts, uncles, cousins, and other close family friends who care for you. Your role in the family circle is to learn, at every stage of your life, how to love in return all the people who love you.

God wants every child He creates to be brought up in a strong family circle where he or she will be loved and cared for at every minute. It doesn't always work that way though, does it? We know that every family has its challenges.

Some families are small, some are very large, some are single-parent families, and even parents who are married to each other don't always agree on every issue. Some families do not have children, some have children with disabilities, some have children they were blessed to adopt, and some have children that do not live with them. Yet, in each of our families, we learn to love in our own unique situation according to God's plan.

Within the circle of family, you will develop the virtues that help you become strong, smart, and pure. Virtues are habits of doing good that help you become a happy woman. Some of the virtues you learn in your family are obedience, honesty, self-control, and thankfulness. Because your parents learned virtues from their parents, and because they practice them throughout their lives, they can teach you about what is right and what is wrong. They have the experience and the desire to help you practice more virtues, such as kindness, patience, courage, and forgiveness, that help you learn how to love. Let's see what virtue Mariana is learning now from her parents to help her become wise and to keep her from growing up too fast.

Mariana's Path to Virtue

Why did Mariana plan a sleepover with her friends when she knew that the autumn dance would be held at her school on the same night? To discover that answer, we need to revisit the hot August day just before the start of middle school . . .

~~~~~~~~~~

"Mariana, your mother and I want to talk to you," her father called from the bottom of the stairs. Mariana jumped up from the chair in her upstairs bedroom where she'd been reading.

"I'm coming, Dad!" she replied as she bounded down the steps.

Her father guided her to the living room where her mother was waiting. Mariana sat down on the soft red couch across from her parents.

"We wanted to talk to you about the school calendar we got in the mail today," her mother began. "There's going to be an autumn dance in September."

Mariana's eyebrows went up. She had never been to a dance before.

"Middle school is not the same as elementary school," said her father. "In junior high, boys and girls often start showing an interest in each other. They might start noticing things about each other that they never noticed before. Some will probably start talking about who likes who in your class. It also sounds like boys will be asking girls to the autumn dance."

Mariana asked, "You mean, boys ask girls to go places on dates in middle school?"

Her father nodded. "Yes, but just because some people are pairing off at this age does not mean your mother and I approve. We believe you should just concentrate on being friends with both girls and boys for now, until you're older."

Her mother nodded and opened the Bible on her lap. "Why don't we read some Scripture verses together and pray about it."

After some time of reading, prayer, and more discussion, Mariana saw the wisdom of her parents. She wasn't even sure if she wanted to go on any dates with boys—at least not yet!

She realized that there was a better path for her to take

during middle school: the way of friendship. Together she and her parents decided that she would hold a sleepover party with a few close girl friends on the night of the dance. Her mother would help her make special snacks, and her mom promised to take the girls roller-skating.

"This is going to be the best sixth grade year ever!" Mariana said with a smile. In her heart, Mariana was happy that her parents prepared her to make that good decision to skip the dance and have her own fun time with her friends at her house.

Celebrate the Friendship Circle

The second circle represents friendship, where you learn what it means to be a good friend and to develop healthy friendships. Because you've learned to give and receive love within your family, now you are able to learn to love people outside that circle.

You don't automatically have friends; friendship is something that must be earned. In order to have friends, you have to *be* a friend. You can't choose your parents or other family members, but you can pick your friends. This is why it's important to choose your friends wisely and learn to make good choices when you're with them.

Within the friendship circle, you learn to express the virtues you've learned in your family: kindness, patience, generosity, respect, and cooperation. You learn to stick up for yourself and for others when necessary and develop additional virtues such as teamwork, leadership, cooperation, and confidence. You'll have many opportunities to stand up for what is right and be a friend to someone who needs one. Maybe a new girl in class is feeling left out; you might reach out in friendship to her and help her to feel welcome. Friends are beautiful gifts from God, and being a friend is a lifelong skill.

Back to Mariana

Mariana had a friend at school named Rosie. One of the boys at school, Kevin, gave a note to Rosie to give to Mariana. Through Rosie, Kevin invited Mariana to the autumn dance. Let's see what happens next . . .

Mariana and Rosie got on the rumbling bus together. They took seats in the back. Once they were settled and the bus began to move, Rosie took Mariana's hand.

"You're so lucky!" she said. Mariana stayed quiet, looking at the green pastures beyond the window. Moments passed before either spoke.

"I don't know . . . ," whispered Mariana.

"Kevin is nice, right?" asked Rosie.

"Yes, he is."

"Kevin is cute, right?" Rosie asked.

"Yes, I guess so."

"You like Kevin, don't you?"

"Well, sorta . . ."

"Mariana, you've just been asked to the dance by the cutest and most popular guy in the school! What else do you need to know?"

Mariana pursed her lips and frowned. "My parents helped me decide not to go to the dance. We agreed that it isn't time for me to start pairing off with boys. That's why we planned the sleepover at my house! You know you were invited, too. Aren't you going to come?"

The bus screeched to a halt at the stop sign where Mariana's street intersected with the main road. As she stood up to get off the bus, Rosie grabbed her sleeve.

"Mariana, you'd be crazy not to go to that dance with Kevin! This is your chance to go out with the most popular guy in school! We can have a sleepover any time we want!"

"Thanks, Rosie. I'll think about it."

Mariana smiled weakly and moved forward along the aisle. She couldn't believe her good friend had just told her to go to the dance when Rosie knew her parents didn't want her to go. Now, she felt really confused.

Discovering Your Real Friends

Friendship love must be earned. We need to learn how to make friends who are trustworthy, who help us become better people. The Bible says, "When you gain friends, gain them through testing, and do not be quick to trust them" (Sir 6:7). Both Mariana and Rosie have been tested by

Kevin's invitation. The test proves what is really inside each of them. By her words, Rosie is showing that she believes it is okay for Mariana to go out with Kevin to the dance, even if that means cancelling the sleepover and disobeying her parents. Her words are temptations for Mariana.

Depending on what she chooses to do, this test might cause Mariana to lose her friendship with Rosie. We'll return to the story a bit later. For now, it's important to realize that every new situation offers a chance for friendships to be tested. In the trials of life, you will find out who your real friends are!

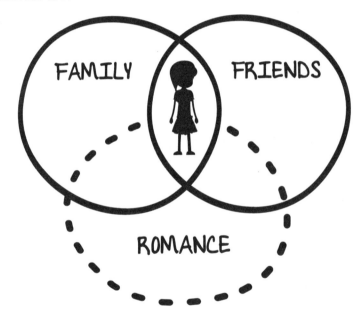

Celebrate the Romance Circle

The third circle is the circle of romantic love, where you can learn about the love you will need for your future marriage. You aren't there yet, but it's good to know about it now so you can prepare for the possibility when you grow up. Before you know it, you will find yourself being attracted to boys. It might even be in the form of having a crush on a popular singer or your coach's assistant. You may want boys to notice you and like you. Boys your age in your neighborhood or school often have funny ways of trying to get a girl's attention. They may show off or tease you. When that happens, it's very important that you practice good manners and don't tease them back. However, if they make fun of you or make jokes about you, it would be good to tell someone who can help them stop. Girls and boys of every age must practice kindness and respect for one another.

The circle of romantic love is a special place to begin to select your marriage partner. It's a place where a woman and a man develop a special kind of friendship. Their friendship begins with discovering common values, hobbies, and interests. They may like reading the same kinds of books or listening to the same style of music. Perhaps they both like pizza but hate tomato sauce. Maybe they both enjoy playing tennis but dislike golf. They may attend the same youth group. They feel a special bond with one another that makes them want to spend more time together.

If you have learned how to be a good friend in the circle of friendship, you will be better prepared to enter the circle of romantic love. In friendships, you learn how to be a virtuous person through being polite, learning good conversation skills, expressing kindness, and being honest and trustworthy. And there are also two new virtues you will need to learn about and practice before you enter the romance circle: modesty and chastity. These virtues help protect your purity in the way you dress, speak, and act around members of the opposite sex. We will talk more about those in a later chapter.

And finally, believe it or not, it's also within this romance circle that you may choose a completely different path: the vocation of religious life, where you will dedicate yourself entirely to God. Religious life is a wonderful, loving choice as well.

Back to Mariana

Will Mariana accept Kevin's invitation to go to the dance? Will she follow the advice of her friend Rosie? Will she disobey her parents by testing the circle of romantic love before she is ready? Let's find out . . .

~~~~~~~~~~

Lost in thought, Mariana walked home slowly, her head down, her feet moving sluggishly. "What should I do," she wondered? She felt a funny, fluttering excitement in her stomach when she thought about Kevin. He had awesome blue eyes and a kind smile. He told jokes that made her laugh. Maybe she did like him after all. Maybe she did want to go to the dance after all. She was embarrassed to tell her parents about the note or about her feelings for Kevin.

When she arrived home, her mother was already in the kitchen, baking.

"You're just in time!" said her mother, stirring the chocolate batter. "Come and help me!"

Mariana put her books and coat away and, putting on an apron, joined her mother in the kitchen. They worked together in silence. Finally Mariana's mother said, "My, you are quiet! Is there something bothering you?"

Mariana shook her head, "No." Her lip began to quiver and tears came to her eyes. "Oh, Mama," she cried. "I don't know what to do!"

Her mother put down the pan of cookies. "Poor girl! I knew something was up! Let's go sit down and talk."

When Mariana had finished telling her mother about the note and what Rosie had said, they hugged each other.

"Mariana," her mother began, "you are such a special young girl, and I'm proud of you for telling me what happened on the school bus today. What do you think you should do?"

Mariana dabbed her eyes with a tissue. "I know I need to do the right thing. I need to stay true to my good decision and have the sleepover with my friends. Besides, Mom, you're right . . . dating is for older boys and girls who are ready to think about marriage. I don't want to think about anything else right now except for school and my friends! Oh, and eating brownies!"

At that, Mariana and her mother laughed.

~~~~~~~~

Parents are a wonderful resource when you're feeling troubled. Sometimes even grandparents or older siblings can help you talk through difficult choices and strong emotions. Chances are, they have experienced exactly the same thing at one time or another! It's good to open up to your parents or other adults you can trust. Remember, the family circle is like a green pasture surrounded by a sturdy fence. Here you are like the little lamb that is protected by the Good Shepherd. The Good Shepherd would never send the lamb out into a storm alone!

In the circle of romantic love, a man and a woman feel physically, emotionally, mentally, and spiritually attracted to each other. In a chaste and respectful way, they explore their unique friendship with one another in order to decide whether or not they want to enter the Sacrament of Marriage as husband and wife.

Smart and Wise

As you go through puberty, your body changes physically from being a girl's body into being a woman's body. As your body changes, your soul grows, too. However, your mind, will, and emotions will grow more slowly than your body because it takes longer to learn good habits of thinking and acting. Puberty is the time to practice good thoughts and actions. It's the time to develop good habits such as the virtues of compassion (love toward others and self), courage (fortitude), and self-control (temperance). During puberty, God wants your soul to become both strong and *smart*.

Most people think that being smart means whizzing through your multiplication tables or memorizing all the state capitals in alphabetical order. But *wisdom* is another kind of "smart," according to the Bible. Have you ever had an aha moment when something puzzling to you suddenly became clear? In a flash, you figured out that stop signs keep cars from running into each other. Or you woke up one morning and realized why you kept missing your homework assignments—you weren't writing them down. These insights come through wisdom, which is the mental ability to gain knowledge or understanding about the world around you.

Yet wisdom is more than just learning from our experiences—it is a supernatural gift given to us by God. The purpose of wisdom is to help you make right choices by knowing what is true and what is false. Wisdom helps you understand God's will and see the right path you need to take. Wisdom isn't a talent you develop—it's a gift you receive. The *Catechism of the Catholic Church* says, "The seven gifts of the Holy Spirit bestowed upon Christians are wisdom, understanding, counsel, fortitude, knowledge, piety, and fear of the Lord" (CCC 1845).

Your soul will grow strong and smart by developing the gift of wisdom within all three circles: family, friendship, and romance.

Being Smart in Your Family

As a daughter, you are a gift to your family. Your mother and father want the very best for you. They want to provide you with food, clothing, shelter, and education. As a daughter, you can develop the good habits of obedience and thankfulness as your loving response for all they do for you. The best way to be obedient is to listen. When your parents ask you to do something, do it promptly and without complaining. If you don't remember what they asked you to do, ask them to repeat their request.

Thankfulness is the habit of saying, "Thank you, Mom" (or Dad or Grandma) and "Thank you, God" for (fill in the blank). The more you thank God for your parents and family, the happier you will feel–and the happier you feel, the easier it will be to obey! Being smart in your family means understanding your role as a sister, too. You have a responsibility to your mom and dad and to your sisters and brothers. If you're an older sister, you may be required to take care of younger siblings. If you're younger, you may be required to obey older siblings when your mom and dad are away from home.

Being Smart in Your Friendships

How can you be smart in your friendships? First, practice habits of virtue that help *you* become the best kind of friend possible. Being a good friend requires wisdom. You're being a good friend when you take turns, play fair, and cooperate. Good friends develop the virtue of honesty by holding one another accountable for being good. Good friends tell the truth and stick up for others. Good friends are polite to adults and respectful of teachers and pastors. Good friends listen rather than talk too much. These are qualities of a good friend. Good friends help us grow in virtue. When you find friends who share your values and love God, they can help you become the best person you can be.

BFFs 4 Ever

Do your friends show those qualities? One way to find out is to ask yourself this question: "When I am around _____ (fill in the name of your friend), am I inspired to be a better person and do the right thing?" If the answer is no, it's time to either find some new friends or help your friends grow in virtue along with you.

The more you leave the family circle for the friendship circle, the more you will discover that love is not as easy to earn. At home you know your parents will love you no matter what. But outside your family, in clubs and sports or in school, you need to learn how to earn the love of others. New social skills are not as hard as learning math or science or history, but they do come more easily for some people and not so easily for others. Becoming a good friend takes practice, too.

Getting Smart about Romance

You can learn about romance now by watching others who live their marriages well. Television shows and movies are often not good examples. Your parents, grandparents, and aunts and uncles may be good role models for romantic relationships. Watching couples treat one another with love and respect will help you learn what it means to be married one day. If you are able to be honest, compassionate, and self-controlled as a friend or daughter, you will be better prepared for having a romantic friendship with a man when you grow up. Being smart means waiting until you are older and knowing yourself well before you enter into a romantic relationship. While you wait to grow in wisdom, you can pray. You can also spend this time getting to know who you are as a unique person, what your strengths and weaknesses are, and learning to know others. Most importantly, you can get to know God, who loves you more than anyone else ever could.

Wrap It Up

Let's review. Your life is surrounded by a big circle that is larger than the universe. This is the first circle that ever existed! This is the circle of God's love. Inside of God's love are three other circles that He created: the circles of family love, friendship love, and romantic love. The family circle provides the safety, protection, and unconditional love you need to develop good habits, or virtues. You can gain wisdom from observing the good role models in your family.

In the circle of friendship, you must earn the love of friends, and they must earn your love as well. Friendships are often tested by difficult decisions or moments. You cannot choose your family, but you can choose your friends. So choose your friends wisely.

The circle of romantic love will be the last circle you enter once your body and soul have been prepared for the responsibilities of marriage and you are ready to make a choice about your vocation.

Wisdom is a gift of the Holy Spirit. Through wisdom you learn to make good choices that enable you to become strong, smart, and pure. During puberty when your body is changing, your soul is growing, too. Puberty is an important time to practice making good choices in your circles of family and friendship.

Discussion Questions

Answer and discuss these questions with your Mom.

1. What do we call the "big circle" that encompasses the other three circles of love? (Hint: It's a WHO, not a what.)

_____

_____

_____

2. Why is wisdom a gift?

_____

_____

_____

3. Why did Mariana's parents think it was best for her to have a girls' overnight party rather than attend the autumn dance?

_____

_____

_____

4. How was Mariana and Rosie's friendship tested? Have you ever had anything like this happen with a friend? How did you resolve it?

_____

_____

_____

5. Why do you and your Mom think it is important to wait, pray, and grow in maturity before entering the circle of romantic love?

_____

_____

_____

Chapter Reflections

While discussing this chapter, my Mom gave me some extra advice about . . .

_____

_____

_____

While reading this chapter, I learned these two important things:

1. _____

2. _____

I resolve to live out the *LoveEd* teachings from this chapter by . . .

_____

_____

_____

Finish this chapter with the following prayer:

God, our Father, you have always been patient with us and good to us. I know that, as a Christian, I need to become more like You. Help me become strong in virtue, one choice at a time, one day at a time. Thank You for always giving me new chances to grow in love for You, for my family, and for my friends. Amen.

My Mom and I completed this chapter on

_____

(date and time)

CHAPTER 3

God Loves Me So Much!

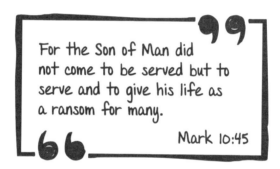

> For the Son of Man did not come to be served but to serve and to give his life as a ransom for many.
>
> Mark 10:45

Did you know that you are "fearfully and wonderfully made?" To be "wonderfully" made means that every part of you, inside and out, has been designed to work together in extraordinary harmony. To be "fearfully made" means to be created in a way that inspires you to shout, "Wow! That is awesome!" The Old Testament poets proclaimed their amazement in Psalm 139: "You formed my inmost being; / you knit me in my mother's womb. / I praise you, because I am wonderfully made; / wonderful are your works!" (Ps 139:13-14).

Once you were created, God didn't stop thinking about you. He thinks about you all the time! He is even thinking about you right now. God loves you more than any human being can. He created you and loves you every day, whether or not you pay attention to Him. "How precious to me are your designs, O God; / how vast the sum of them! / Were I to count them, they would outnumber the sands; / when I complete them, still you are with me" (Ps 139:17-18).

Your life is a gift from God! The writer of Psalm 139 tells us that God made each human being purposefully and exceptionally for a reason. He gave you a body and a soul so you might live all of your days on earth loving Him and loving others. God wants you to use your gifts and talents to help others. Maybe you will be a teacher when you grow up, taking care of a classroom of twenty kindergarten students. Perhaps you will be the leader of a major company, caring for thousands of employees. God has given you a life with many stages in it. Puberty and adolescence is a time to learn about and develop your special talents and gifts so you can make your life a gift to God while serving others.

Growing Up in God's Plan

During puberty and adolescence, your body and soul prepare for a loving adulthood. There are two primary vocations a girl can choose when she is an adult: marriage and motherhood or the religious life. A woman may also choose to remain single and serve God in other ways. No matter what you might be when you grow up, God has programmed every female body with the potential to bring new life into the world. God planned for you to be a girl so that your body would be able to carry a baby someday, if and when you are ready to become a loving wife and mother.

Whatever your vocation, God also planned that you grow a beautiful soul full of virtues. Raising children and serving others in society requires a lot of patience and wisdom—virtues you are learning now as a preteen.

You may decide that you want to serve God by becoming a religious sister. If you say yes to God, you will develop a personal prayer life that brings you very close to God. You will spend your life in a religious order with other women who have also said yes to God in a special and holy way. You will bring God's love and compassion into the lives of others, especially the poor, the sick, and the uneducated.

Growing into an adult is part of life and part of God's plan. God wants you to share your unique gifts with the world to make the world a better place. You have the next ten years or so to think about that. Ask yourself, *what gifts did God give me? What will I make of my life as a gift back to Him?*

What Is Life All About?

When you stare out your bedroom window, you may think about the same things human beings always think about: *Why did God make me? What does human life really mean? What am I here for? Is life just for fun, or is there something more? How will God help me through this life? How can I make sure I will be with Him for all eternity? Why does sin look like fun for some people? Is life a scary adventure or a happy adventure? Why is there sadness and suffering sometimes? Where do I fit in this universe? How do I grow up to be happy with God?*

As you learn more in school, at church, and in life, you will begin to think new and different thoughts. You will start to wonder about the meaning of life and your purpose for being on earth. You'll start thinking more about what you will do when you grow up. You wonder if you will be married someday and become a mother. You will start asking more questions about everything. Eventually, you'll look beyond your family for friends and role models. This is all normal; it's part of the growing-up process. And since human beings have been asking themselves these questions from the beginning, there are some answers. Actually,

God has all the answers. We just need to stay close to Him, study more about Him so we can love Him more, and listen to Him in order to learn how to live and love.

The Story of Us

Life is an adventure that began long before you were born. Before your parents and your grandparents. Before Abe Lincoln and George Washington. Before Joan of Arc and Shakespeare. Before Homer, the Vikings, and cavemen.

Before anything existed, there was God. God made the whole world, and He made it amazing. He filled the sky full of stars. He made snow fall on mountaintops that soar above the clouds. He made oceans and rushing rivers and forests of giant trees. God is the ultimate scientist, having written the laws of the universe. And God is the ultimate artist, having set the standard for beauty.

The world He made was big and beautiful, but it wasn't enough for Him. God wanted to share His life and love even more. So He made us. We are God's greatest idea, God's artistic masterpiece. Our bodies and souls, our hearts and minds are all a reflection of God's greater being.

Our whole purpose for being is to love one another and to give our lives back to the God who gave us everything—everything we are, everything we see. When God created us, He gave every human being two great gifts that make us capable of loving: the ability to know and the power to make free choices.

He took a great risk in giving us such amazing gifts as intelligence and free will. We could choose to use our freedom and intelligence for Him or against Him. And right from the beginning, the human race failed to follow God's plan. With our ability to know, we said that we knew better and challenged God's plan. With our power to choose, we chose our own selfish desires and rejected God's love.

This is the reality we call sin. Sin is a choice to turn away from God. Sin goes against the beauty and order of God's creation because whenever we choose not to follow God's plan, we choose not to love. Our unloving choices have bad consequences for ourselves and for everyone around us.

When we are children, our parents try to protect us from all harmful things. That's why your parents have certain rules for you and make choices for you when you are a child. But they can't protect you forever. The older you get, the more temptations you'll face. You need a lot of courage to resist the pressure to sin and a lot of grace each day to choose to do what is right. As you grow up, you'll notice more good and more evil than you did when you were a child. You will see the world differently. Why is this so? It's due to original sin, the sin that all people inherited from Adam and Eve that keeps us from loving one another perfectly and being happy with God all the time.

In the beginning, when God created Adam and Eve, God's plan was perfect. Marriage and family were designed to be fulfilling for men, women, and children. It was designed so that everyone would be happy with each other and in perfect union with God. But something happened that changed that perfect life: a free will act of disobedience—the original sin of Adam and Eve.

Man and woman fell for Satan's lies. "You will be like God," the Devil said. After they committed original sin, their perfect life was wounded and would never be the same. They no longer lived in harmony and selfless love; they became confused about the nature and purpose of their bodies and their lives, and they were tempted to use one another out of selfishness.

Pope Francis once called the Devil a con artist—a liar who only succeeds by fooling people. "He makes promise after promise, but he never delivers," said the pope. "He'll never really do anything he says. He doesn't make good on his promises. He makes you want things which he can't give, whether you get them or not. He makes you put your hopes in things which will never make you happy. That's his game, his strategy. He talks a lot, he offers a lot, but he doesn't deliver."

Because of original sin, people chose to sin rather than to be with God. But in reality we become unhappy when we sin, because we cannot be truly happy without God, who is love. Thus, God knew we needed a savior.

So, out of His great mercy and love, God sent His Son, Jesus Christ, to make up for Adam and Eve's sin and for all of our sins so we can live in peace and harmony when we follow His way of love and live a moral life. God's perfect plan was broken by original sin and redeemed by Jesus Christ. Jesus came to earth to show us what God's love is like. And when Jesus died for us, He showed us the ultimate act of love. He taught us that love is always greater than our sin. It is through this love that God redeemed creation.

By His sacrifice of death on the Cross, Jesus made all things new again. This act shows us a God who never stops loving us, never gives up on us. When we sin, God always gives us another chance to come home to Him and ask for forgiveness. This is why Jesus gave us the Sacrament of Reconciliation. God wants us to experience His forgiveness whenever we're sorry for our sins and confess them. He wants us to be filled with His grace, which is His life and love inside of us.

God knows that other people's sins affect us, too. This brings sadness into the world. But God doesn't give up on us then, either. When we're wounded by another person's sin, God sends someone to bring us the healing power of His love. He may send His love through a parent, a friend, a relative, or a counselor. God always has help for us, and He can sometimes directly answer us and heal us through our prayers. Mercy and healing are ways that God shows us His love directly. And when we're confronted by painful situations, we always have the power to choose to love because we have His grace and strength in us through baptism. God lives with you and in you.

Jesus doesn't lie to us like the Devil does. Jesus shows us that we can live on His path of life, love, and truth by following the commandments, living the virtues, and loving others in a good and holy way.

And now it's our turn. Now it's up to us to bring forth God's love—to overcome sin and help create a loving world.

How are you going to do that?

By learning to love others in all your circles of life and throughout all the changes taking place within you. Because of God's grace, you can learn to be kind and patient and merciful and forgiving to others, even when you don't *feel* like it.

As long as you are on this earth, you will always face temptations. As you grow, you will experience the tug-of-war between choosing right and choosing wrong. Temptations will test your faith in various ways. But the Bible reminds us that the "testing of your faith produces perseverance" (Jas 1:3), helping you grow into a mature person. Your faith, your family, and your good friends are here to support you and cheer you on, guiding you to be the good person God has chosen you to be.

Be Spiritually and Emotionally Strong

Spiritual strength is available to us through the sacraments, prayer, and our connection to the Church. When you're going through a tough time, whether it's a time of temptation or a time of confusion, here are some things you can do to help you become spiritually stronger:

- Pray to God and ask Him to shed light on what you should do.
- Ask God to carry your burdens; He will!
- Sing some songs of praise to God and enjoy being with Him.
- Spend some time out in nature, and thank God for creating our world.
- Exercise, hike, or go running outdoors while thinking about God—it can clear your head and fill you with His beauty and love.
- Find ways to help others, such as washing your neighbor's car, mowing the lawn, or babysitting for friends at church.
- Set yourself a goal of doing a certain number of good deeds for the day. Practicing God's love in that way actually helps you while you're helping others.

A Crazy Three-Ring Circus

How do I become strong and smart about God's love? How do I become pure in living His love? To answer that question, let's see how Mariana is doing. It's the following September, and the entire year of sixth grade has passed! Mariana is now entering seventh grade.

It was the Saturday night of the traditional autumn dance at Mariana's middle school, and Mariana was so excited she could barely sit still.

"Mom, when will the brownies be ready?" she asked, bouncing up and down on the balls of her feet.

"Now, hold on!" said her mother. "I know you're excited about having your girl buddies come over for a slumber party, but if you don't want chocolate goo, you'll need to wait until these finish baking!"

Mariana's father walked into the kitchen, carrying his leather bag with his special green bowling ball in it.

"Mariana, I'm so glad you decided to have a slumber party instead of going to the dance," her father said, tousling her hair with one hand.

Mariana beamed. "I couldn't do it without your help, Mom!"

The doorbell rang. "It's them!" yelled Mariana, running to the door. Rosie, Natalia, Francine, and Becky had carpooled together to Mariana's house, and when she opened the door, they rushed in with their sleeping bags, pillows, and suitcases. "This is going to be a fun time," thought Mariana.

First her father took them all to the bowling alley for some friendly competition, followed by a drive-by pizza-pick-up from Torino's Pizzeria. Filled with pizza, they still found room for brownies, potato chips, and soda.

Finally, too full to move, the girls stretched out on their sleeping bags in the living room. Before going to sleep,

Mariana's parents came in to read the Bible and say their nightly prayers.

"Any prayer requests?" asked Mariana's mother.

Becky raised her hand. "Yes," she said nervously. "Please pray for my mom and dad. I think they might be, well, splitting up . . . and I don't want them to get a divorce!" She began to cry.

The other girls gathered around Becky and hugged her. Francine cleared her throat and squeaked out a few words, "Please pray for my brother—he and his girlfriend broke up."

Before the group could begin to pray, Rosie spoke up. "I have a prayer need, too," she said. "Please pray for my sister, Anne. She's in college, and, well . . . she doesn't go to church anymore." Rosie's face turned red as tears began to fall down her cheeks.

Natalia rubbed Rosie's arm affectionately. "I know how you feel," she said. "My mom stopped going to church, too."

Francine suddenly sat up straight on her pink sleeping bag. "At my house, we have a two-year-old toddler, a baby puppy, and a cranky big sister! It's like a crazy three-ring circus!" Everyone laughed for a moment before the room became quiet and serious again.

Mariana hesitated, then spoke up. "I have a different kind of prayer—it's a thank you prayer." She took a deep breath. "Thank you, God, that my friend Rosie decided to skip the dance this year so she could come to the slumber party with us. And thank you for these special friends here with me tonight."

Mariana's mother looked lovingly at each of the girls and said, "My, we do have some prayer needs, don't we?"

Mr. Garcia said, "Why don't we pray the Rosary together? We need the intercession of our Blessed Mother Mary."

For the next twenty minutes, they prayed the Rosary, their voices trembling and weak, but growing stronger as they felt the loving presence of God infuse their hearts.

Prayer Helps Us to Love

Do you have friends who are hurting? Is something in your own life causing you to suffer? Like Mariana and her friends, you are not alone in your troubles! Here on earth, trials and difficulties come to everyone at different times. When facing troubled times, praying to God helps us get stronger on the inside.

When you pray, you're training your mind to focus on God instead of your problems or temptations. You're learning to turn to God for everything you need. You're getting closer to the God who loves you. You fill up with His love so you can give it to others. When you choose to help others instead of being selfish, you become more mature and more cheerful, too. These changes during puberty that you are experiencing are all part of a good process—a process designed by God to help you mature.

Keeping Your Love for God Pure

To be pure at heart means seeing the true value of those around you. People always said that when St. John Paul II or St. Teresa of Calcutta looked at them, they felt special, as though they were the only people in the world. That's purity of heart. Holy people have a way of seeing the importance of everyone they meet. When you meet someone holy, that person makes you understand not just how good they are, but you learn a little bit about how good *you* are, too.

We all need to be pure at heart. You need to see the people in your family as important and worth your best. You need to think of your friends and the people you meet at school as special people, deserving the best you can give them. Remember that each person is made with the dignity of God and deserves respect.

Strengthened to Live God's Love

Showing God that you love Him with a pure heart requires being virtuous. If you build the virtues in your soul now, you will be happy later. If you ignore them, you will have a much more difficult time in life. You will be challenged daily to choose virtues that reflect God's great love by making one good choice at a time.

It's your job right now, as a growing young woman, to practice building your character and virtue each day so you can become the woman God wants you to be. You will need years of practicing the virtues with courtesy and respect for others in order to be a good wife and mother, religious sister, or single woman. *Everyone* needs to be strong in virtue.

Four fundamental virtues are called the cardinal virtues—practicing these virtues lays the foundation for all the others.

- **Prudence** is being cautious and thinking before you speak or act. If you want to avoid getting caught in a sticky situation that will lead you to sin, develop the virtue of prudence by making good decisions starting now. Lead yourself not into temptation.
- **Justice** is doing what's right and fair, giving to God what is owed to Him, and giving to others what they are due. It means being truthful with your parents, fair with your friends, and honest with yourself.

Obedience is part of justice because obeying God and your parents is fair; it is what is owed to them.

- **Fortitude** is having the "guts" to say no to something you know is wrong. It's having the courage to resist evil and do good and the mental and emotional strength necessary to face and combat difficulty, adversity, danger, or temptation.

- **Temperance** is a very practical virtue that helps you balance your life by using moderation. Temperance is self-restraint in actions, such as speaking, eating, drinking, or playing. Temperance is all about using self-control. Temperance helps you train your will to win over your impulses and feelings so that you can turn all your desires toward what is good—no matter what you *feel* like doing. Temperance also includes the virtue of modesty in dress, words, and behavior.

The cardinal virtues are spiritual strengths designed to help you stay on the track to happiness and real love.

Mary, Our Model of Virtue, Purity, and Beauty

The role model for all women is Mary, the mother of Jesus, who loved God with a pure and undivided heart. Mary always said yes to God's will. Mary was only a teenager when the angel Gabriel appeared to her and asked her to be the mother of Jesus. Mary didn't exactly know what that would mean for her life, but she said, "May it be done to me according to your word" (Lk 1:38). We can think about Mary's obedience when we pray the first Joyful Mystery of the Rosary: the Annunciation.

We know that Mary was kind and thoughtful toward

others. After the angel told her that her cousin Elizabeth was pregnant in her old age, Mary set out right away to visit her cousin. We can think about Mary's kindness when praying the second Joyful Mystery of the Rosary: the Visitation.

Mary was strong in virtue and inner strength, even in the face of the many hardships in her life. She had to travel to Bethlehem and give birth to Jesus in a stable. Mary delivered Jesus, the Son of God, to all of us. If we stay close to Mary, our spiritual mother, she will continue to bring us to her Son, Jesus Christ.

It's important to pray the Rosary often during this time of puberty and adolescence. This form of prayer will help you stay close to Mary and Jesus. Mary was a teenager once too, and she is now your heavenly mother who wants to help you and guide you.

God created Mary to be a beautiful woman, just as He created *all* women to be beautiful, each in their own special way. God wants each woman to reflect His beauty to the world. This beauty of the soul is not the same as the beauty you might read about in the ads for makeup, jewelry, and hair products. God's beauty is the inner beauty that shines through when you are pure and doing His will. Inner beauty is true beauty. Living out the virtues, women can be mirrors or reflections of God's love. As you grow in virtue, people will see God's love and goodness in you; they will see the goodness of God alive in the world today. "You are the light of the world. A city set on a mountain cannot be hidden. . . . Just so, your light must shine before others, that they may see your good deeds and glorify your heavenly Father" (Mt 5:14, 16).

Just as we can see the love and beauty of God in His creation of the world, He wants people to see the love and the beauty of His creation in you.

Wrap It Up

Puberty will bring many changes in the way you look, act, and think. This is all part of God's plan for you, and you will grow in maturity through it while you develop the virtues. Personal prayer is an important part of life to help you stay strong and close to God.

God has a plan for all human beings to share His love with the world. God loves you, and He created you to love. Due to original sin, we sometimes choose our own way rather than God's way. Jesus redeemed us and saved us from the punishment for sin. He gives us the grace we need to avoid sin and resist temptation.

The cardinal virtues are important strengths we need to develop in order to grow in God's love.

The Blessed Virgin Mary is our model for virtue, purity, and inner beauty.

Discussion Questions

1. Complete this exercise with your Mom:

In one minute, make a separate list of all the gifts God has given you.

_____

_____

_____

_____

Now, take two minutes to write down what you can give as a gift back to God.

_____

_____

_____

_____

Discuss your lists together for three minutes: What are you giving back to God now, and what do you plan to give back to God in the future?

_____

_____

_____

_____

2. Ask yourself these questions about your spiritual life. Write down any helpful thoughts you might have that you would like to review later.

What is your prayer routine? Do you pray when you get up? When you go to bed?

_____

_____

_____

_____

What is your favorite story from the Bible? What do you like about it?

_____

_____

_____

_____

Is there anything you have a hard time talking to God about?

_____

_____

_____

_____

When was your last confession? Are there things you want to confess so God can heal them? Are you in need of God's mercy and forgiveness? Are there some regular habits of sin you are trying to stop? Do you have a plan to avoid them?

_____

_____

_____

_____

Do you remind yourself about the Real Presence of Jesus when you receive Communion?

_____

_____

_____

_____

Do you know how to pray the Rosary? How often do you pray the Rosary? Do you know the twenty different mysteries to meditate on during the decades of the Rosary? What is your favorite mystery of the Rosary?

_____

_____

_____

_____

Chapter Reflections

While discussing this chapter, my Mom gave me some extra advice about . . .

_____

_____

_____

While reading this chapter, I learned these two important things:

1. _____

2. _____

I resolve to live out the *LoveEd* teachings from this chapter by . . .

_____

_____

_____

Finish this chapter with the following prayer:

Dear Jesus, thank You for coming into this world to redeem us. Thank You for showing us how to live and how to love. I ask that You keep giving me the grace to be better each day. I want to make this world a better place to live in order to give You glory. Amen.

My Mom and I completed this chapter on

_____

(date and time)

CHAPTER 4

Becoming a Woman

> My soul proclaims the greatness of the Lord; my spirit rejoices in God my savior. For he has looked upon his handmaid's lowliness; behold, from now on will all ages call me blessed. The Mighty One has done great things for me, and holy is his name.
>
> Luke 1:46–49

Changing from the Inside Out

God created Adam and Eve as the first man and woman; the first husband and wife. Since the Garden of Eden, the family has been designed to include a biological mother and father and any children they have together. "God blessed them and God said to them: Be fertile and multiply; fill the earth and subdue it" (Gn 1:28).

God's plan from the beginning was for one man and

one woman to join together in the covenant of marriage in order to cocreate new human life with Him. In the Catholic Church, we call this the Sacrament of Marriage. "That is why a man leaves his father and mother and clings to his wife, and the two of them become one body" (Gn 2:24). You came into existence because of the love of your parents and the love of God.

When God created Adam and Eve, He made them to unite their lives to create a family and to fill the earth with people who can share God's love. The purpose of the family is to be the "heart" of society, since it is within that first circle that we learn to love and share love with others. Without the heart, a body cannot live. Without strong Christian families, the society around us will become weak and sick. In the family circle, you can discover the heart of God, who shares His love with you through your family.

What You Can Expect During Puberty

God placed this plan for families within our hearts and wrote it within our very bodies. During puberty, a girl's body begins to change into a woman's body, and a boy's body begins to change into a man's. This prepares them to one day get married and have children. Their bodies, emotions, minds, and hearts are also prepared for God's plan. So all of this physical growth is not just something to "put up with"; it's part of God's plan for men and women.

The changes of puberty begin in your brain, where your pituitary gland sends out a female hormone called estrogen. In boys, the main hormone is called testosterone. Everyone is born with these naturally occurring chemicals in their bodies. These hormones are produced and sent out by the endocrine and reproductive systems. Hormones send signals to various organs of the body to grow and change.

These changes occur gradually and are part of God's plan to prepare your body for adulthood. During puberty, the increased hormones cause your sexual organs to grow, as well as your whole body. The inside changes at puberty occur mostly in your reproductive organs, which are located below the stomach and just above the hips. Your outside changes can be seen in the changing shape and size of your body. Your hips widen, your waist gets smaller, and your breasts begin to grow. We will discuss these changes in more detail later in this chapter.

Puberty usually lasts about four years. For girls, the average age to begin puberty is thirteen, but anytime between the ages of nine and sixteen is considered normal. Boys begin puberty between the ages of eleven and seventeen, with the average age being fourteen.

God designed puberty so that one day you could possibly bring new human life into the world when you are married. Not every person will be married, and not everyone will have children. Yet all bodies are designed by God to have *the potential* of creating new life in adulthood.

Outside Changes

Breast growth. One of the first changes a girl may notice is the growth of her breasts. Small buds begin to form on your chest, underneath the skin behind the nipples. The breast buds may feel hard or tender, but soon soften as the breasts grow. Inside your breasts, the mammary glands are developing and getting ready to someday produce milk in order to feed a baby if you become a mother. When you see signs of breast growth, talk to your mom about wearing a bra. Wearing a bra is important for modesty and protection as soon as your breasts begin to grow. Breast development happens differently for every girl. The shape and size of your breasts are unique, just as you are unique. Trust that God has made you in a special way, so don't compare yourself with other girls.

Changing shape. Your hips will widen to prepare your body for carrying a baby one day. Your waist will become thinner. Your legs and arms will get longer and more defined. You will lose your baby fat as you continue to grow taller and curvier. Your facial bones will take on a softer shape, and you will look prettier. You will not just be "cute" like a little girl; you will be beautiful like a woman.

Skin changes. Your hair and body may become oilier because of all the hormones going through your system. Some girls will struggle with acne during this time. Hair will begin to grow on your legs and underarms. Pubic hair also grows between your legs, covering the skin folds called labia near the outer part of the vagina.

Inside Changes

Reproductive system. This is the system that allows you to one day reproduce, which means create new human life with God and your future husband. A girl's reproductive organs are on the inside, above her hips and below her stomach. Here is a list of the female reproductive organs:

Ovaries. These are two almond-shaped organs on either side of the uterus (also called the womb). Your ovaries are filled with very tiny egg cells, called ovum, which will mature later, usually one at a time.

Fallopian tubes. These are connected to the ovaries; these short tubes or passageways help move the egg cells from the ovaries towards the uterus each month.

Uterus (womb). This muscular organ is in the inside center of your body, between your hips and just below your belly button. It rests below the ovaries and fallopian tubes, just above the vagina. The uterus is normally about the size and shape of a pear. It is the place where a baby grows within the mother during pregnancy. The uterus is made of thick muscle tissue that stretches around the baby as it grows bigger and bigger each month during the nine months of pregnancy.

Cervix. This is the small opening between the uterus and the vagina. Each month it opens just enough for the monthly menstrual flow to exit from the uterus into the vagina. During the birth process it can stretch around a baby to let the baby out through to the vagina.

Vagina (birth canal). The vagina is a short muscular organ that connects the uterus to the outside of your body. It is also called the birth canal since it is the passageway for the baby to leave the mother's body after it has grown for nine months in the uterus. When a mother gives birth, the muscular contractions of the uterus push the baby out through the cervix and vagina, which stretch around the baby as it passes through.

Menstruation

Every month, a woman goes through a natural process called menstruation. The word comes from the Latin term *menses*, which means "month." Also called a "period," it comes in a regular pattern about every twenty-eight days or so. Menstruation is a normal process that lasts for three to seven days each month. Once menstruation starts during puberty, it will happen every month until a woman is about fifty years old, except during the nine months of pregnancy. For the first year or two, while your body's system is settling into a routine, your periods may be irregular. Eventually, if you keep track on a calendar, you will see a more predictable cycle.

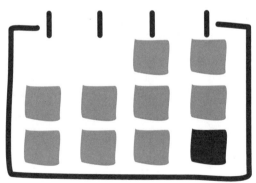

Before you have your first period, your pituitary gland will release hormones that are carried by your bloodstream to your ovaries. Then, once a month, one egg cell will mature and be released by the ovary into the fallopian tube. At that same time of the month, the uterus prepares a soft lining of nutrient-rich blood and fluid for a possible pregnancy. If pregnancy does not occur, the egg will dissolve as it passes through the uterus. This is the body's cue to release the nutrient-rich lining. The lining of blood will be released slowly from the uterus. The release of the blood and fluid through the vagina to the outside of the body is called menstruation or, more simply, "having your period." A small amount—about half of a cup—will flow out very slowly over several days. Sometimes it flows in drops, in a gentle release, and sometimes it comes out in thicker red clots. Some girls and women may experience achy feelings called cramps in their lower abdomen just before or during their period, but the menstrual flow itself does not hurt.

Some women feel cranky or tired just before their period. You will probably not notice when the egg cell releases, or even know it is happening on the inside. But you will definitely notice and feel the menstrual flow! You will know your period may be coming in a week or so when you see a little yellowish-white discharge in your underwear. The next sign (usually the day before your period) might be a little spotting of blood on your underwear. Sometimes a girl will want to wear panty liners a few days before her period starts. On the days of her period, she'll need to wear a protective sanitary napkin. Talk to your mom about the right size and brand of pads for you, and have her show you how to place them properly in your underwear.

Ask your mother to help you make a list of special feminine products you need during puberty. Your list may include deodorant, mild soap, and sanitary pads. If you're a swimmer or an athlete, there may be a time when your mom will want to teach you how to use tampons to absorb the menstrual flow in a different way. You might also like to treat yourself to a few "luxuries," such as a little bag of chocolates, a soft heating pad, or a citrus body splash! Clean out a drawer in your dresser and keep all of your special and private feminine items there.

Personal hygiene is important during your period. You will need to learn how to change your sanitary pads regularly, usually every few hours when you go to the bathroom. It will be important to keep your private area clean during your period. You may want to carry an extra pad in your purse or backpack for emergencies. If you ever feel or notice something about your body during menstruation that concerns you, talk with a trusted woman, like your mom, sister, grandmother, or a female teacher. They can help you know what is normal and help you find health and wellness assistance if necessary.

If you get your first period while you're at school, you can go to a female teacher, the school nurse, or the school secretary; tell them you just got your period and ask for a sanitary pad. They usually keep a secret supply just for girls on those days, so don't be embarrassed to ask them. Menstruation is something all women understand. They also know it might come at times you are unprepared.

Your period signals that your body is getting ready for womanhood. There may be other slightly noticeable times of moisture during the monthly cycle as well. These are various signs of fertility in your monthly cycle that you will learn about before you're married so that you can use natural family planning with your husband.

Starting your menstrual cycle is just one step in the

grand adventure of growing up and becoming a woman. It only takes a few months to adjust to this new monthly occurrence. You will soon become responsible enough to manage your cleanliness and personal hygiene on your own. Managing your emotions will be a new adventure, too. God wants you to grow emotionally, mentally, and spiritually during puberty.

Celebrate Your Femininity!

What is femininity? It is the expression of your "femaleness," both on the outside and on the inside. There are biological traits unique to females, and we call those a woman's femininity.

Men and women think differently, they process their emotions differently, and they see people differently. Girls usually walk and talk differently than boys. Research has shown that women say at least three times as many words per day than boys do. Your femininity is not just in what you say; it's also expressed inside your mind and heart.

God made boys to be biologically, physically, and emotionally different than girls. He created human beings as two different genders: male and female. Boys and girls are just different, even though they sometimes have the same hobbies, talents, and gifts. Girls can be athletic and build their muscles by lifting weights or running races. But because of the hormone testosterone, boys have the advantage of thicker muscles, denser bones, and increased physical strength. On the other hand, research shows that girls develop their language skills sooner than boys, which often makes them good at reading, writing, and spelling. *Even when boys and girls are good at doing the same things, that doesn't change their gender.* God created each person male or female.

Girls often enjoy spending time together doing those things boys don't usually enjoy. For example, boys like tackling and crashing into each other more than girls do. Maybe that's why football was invented! Boys like to get muddy and catch frogs more than girls do, yet some girls enjoy that too. Girls may join more dance camps, cooking clubs, spelling bees, or craft classes than boys. Girls may become cheerleaders or volleyball players, while boys may join the all-male basketball team as they get taller. As girls grow into women, they continue to look for friendships with one another. College girls hang out in their dorms, moms may join groups for preschool mothers, and career singles may join an all-female business organization.

By spending time with your female friends, you will discover your God-given uniqueness and beauty. By spending time with their male friends, boys will discover their God-given traits and masculinity. Even though it's good to have both male and female friends, you'll find that spending time with just "the girls" is important, whether it's your teammates, sisters, cousins, or just you and your mom. An occasional girls night out is something all women enjoy. You'll find that only in a group of girls or women can you share tips and ideas about some of the "girl stuff" that you all go through.

Every girl dreams of growing up to become someone wonderful. Some girls dream about becoming president of the United States! Others want to become doctors, nurses, or teachers. You may have friends who want to be dancers or artists or writers when they grow up. Many little girls dream about getting married one day and having children. A few girls answer the call to the religious life, becoming nuns like St. Thérèse of Lisieux or Mother Teresa. As a preteen, you can have fun dreaming about all the wonderful things you can do when you grow up!

Dressing with Dignity

Preteen girls going through puberty often have fun shopping for the new clothes they will need to fit their changing bodies—and Mariana is no different! Today, her mother is taking her shopping for new clothes to wear during the spring semester at school:

~~~~~~~~~

"Let's try this store," said Mariana's mother.

Together, Mariana and her mother walked through the big doors of the fancy boutique in the middle of downtown. Mariana felt overwhelmed as she looked around at all of the beautiful clothing and shoes. A friendly sales clerk approached them.

"May I help you?" she asked. The woman wore a baby-blue shirt and a navy blue jacket and skirt. Her hair was brushed and curled, and she had nicely painted fingernails. She looked very professional, yet feminine.

"Yes," answered Mariana's mother. "We need some nice skirts and blouses for my daughter to wear in the spring."

The woman nodded and led them to the back of the store. "Here we have some very cute things in your size," she said. "Perhaps you'd like something like this?"

The woman showed Mariana a beautiful light-orange shirt with a collar and a matching multicolor striped skirt. Her mother selected a pair of slip-on patent leather shoes and a silver necklace with a heart-shaped locket.

"Wouldn't these look nice on you, too?" she said. Mariana beamed. She felt like a lady as she walked into the dressing room. She put on the clothing, and then walked out to show her mother.

"You look beautiful, Mariana!" said her mother.

The helpful saleswoman nodded. "She's right. You look awesome!"

Mariana felt beautiful on the inside and the outside. She twirled around in the skirt, which felt light and comfortable and came down to just above her knees. She liked how she looked! She liked growing up!

Growing girls like Mariana can try out new, feminine accessories, clothing, and products. Puberty is the time when mothers may let their daughters wear simple jewelry or a little makeup. Each mother decides what's best for her own daughter. The most important part of picking out a new wardrobe is finding modest clothing.

Modesty is a virtue that helps you dress and behave like a lady and reminds men and other women to treat you with respect. A lady carries herself with dignity and confidence. She wears clothing that conceals her private parts and doesn't distract the eyes of others. A lady acts modestly when she speaks with kindness, refrains from lashing out in anger, and uses her voice—rather than her body—to communicate with others. When you wear attractive and decent clothing, you're saying you are proud to be a child of God; you're proud to be a girl who's on her way to becoming a virtuous and beautiful woman!

We live in a culture today that doesn't always respect true femininity, and many girls struggle with self-image and self-respect. Some people don't understand their dignified role as women or the way in which God planned for men to treasure and respect them. Hollywood movies and popular music portray women's bodies as objects for men's pleasure. Both fashion trends and peer pressure can push girls to buy immodest clothing so they will look "sexy" and desirable. Some girls show off the womanly parts of their bodies by exposing too much of their legs or bellies or breasts. The unfortunate result is that people remember them for their bodies rather than their talents and virtues.

But there is a better way; it's called "dressing with dignity." By choosing modest clothing, simple makeup, and pretty jewelry, you're expressing your God-given dignity and protecting the special feminine parts of your body. Modesty gives you feelings of self-worth and self-respect. When you wear attractive, modest clothing, you're saying you are proud to be a child of God and confident enough to be your total self without having to conform to what society says about how a woman should look.

Managing Your Emotions

During puberty it's normal to experience many strong emotions that are both positive and negative. You may enjoy feelings of excitement, playfulness, attraction, confidence, and satisfaction. Other emotions may be negative or painful, such as sadness, discouragement, rejection, fear, frustration, or crankiness. Feeling "blue" or irritable can drag you down if you let it. You may find yourself changing moods more often during puberty than you used to. Sometimes you won't even know why you feel the way that you do.

All negative feelings do not have to be acted out, but it's not good to "bury them" or stuff them inside, either. You can learn to manage and accept your feelings for what they are—merely indicators of pleasure or pain. When you experience them, you should think: *How should I act in response to these feelings in a way that would help myself and others?* Then you can pray, "How would God want me to act?"

You can use your mind and your free will to practice managing your feelings in many new, more grown-up ways. Little children might throw tantrums when they are mad or frustrated because they don't know how to express themselves well. Now that you're older, you can practice self-control over your behavior no matter what you are feeling. You should feel, think, pray, and then act in the most loving way possible. Feel, think, pray—then act.

Have you ever gone swimming in the ocean? If so, you know that sometimes the waves and currents can become large and powerful. If you want to swim back to the beach, you have to work hard against the choppy waters. This takes perseverance, especially when you feel too tired to kick your legs and move your arms. Your emotions during puberty may feel just like those vigorous waves of the ocean—so strong that you feel you can't push back! But just as you must tell yourself to swim back to the beach, you can also tell yourself to use your inner strength to manage the powerful emotions washing over you. Remember that you are strong with God's grace inside of you. You can overcome negative emotions by making a decision in your mind and your will and then choosing to act in the proper way when you express them. This is what we call self-control.

Learn how to manage your emotions by thinking first before you act. Think about what the right thing to do might be. Emotions can be managed without hurting others or yourself. Good physical health, good exercise, good friends, and the support of your family can help you learn to experience both good and bad emotions well. Here are a few more ways that will help you do this:

- Talk about your feelings with your parents or friends.
- Exercise—it increases the "happy hormone" in your brain.
- Do some hard work—helping clean out the garage or planting a garden for example.
- Express yourself through music, dancing, writing, or art.
- Find a hobby that interests you, such as painting, skateboarding, or chess.

These are all good ways to express your emotional energy.

Wrap It Up

Puberty is part of God's beautiful plan for a young girl's body to develop into a beautiful woman's body. Puberty is not just physical; it also includes the growth and development of your emotions, your intelligence, and your spirituality. Remember, puberty is not simply happening *to* you—puberty is a time in your life when you learn how to *take charge* of your body, your emotions, and your soul.

Taking charge means having self-control. The Holy Spirit will grow the fruit of self-control within you when you pray for it. Your job is to exercise self-control in the difficult moments of your life. Instead of shouting at your brother when you're angry, pray for the courage to hold your tongue and work things out peacefully. As you grow up, you will have many chances to practice self-control and other virtues. Chastity and modesty are also very important virtues to practice—from how you act and talk to how you dress. Becoming strong and smart is a lifelong process, but it starts now. As you develop healthy, holy habits during puberty, you will be participating in God's special plan for you and bring glory to God!

Discussion Questions

Answer and discuss these questions with your Mom.

1. What are some of the changes you can expect to happen during puberty?

_____

_____

_____

2. Why does puberty happen and how does it begin? Is puberty happening to you right now?

_____

_____

_____

3. What are hormones?

_____

_____

_____

4. Name the organs in your reproductive system and review with your Mom what their function is. Look back at the diagram in Act 4 if you need help.

_____

_____

_____

5. When does a woman's body begin to produce milk? (check one)

☐ only after a baby is born
☐ as soon as her mammary glands develop
☐ the day she gets married
☐ when she starts to wear a bra

6. What is true and false about menstruation? (write T or F)

☐ It's a monthly release of the lining of the uterus.
☐ It happens 3-7 days a month from puberty to menopause.
☐ It's when the hip bones widen.
☐ It occurs when a mom is pregnant.

7. What are the signs of your period starting?

_____

_____

_____

8. What is femininity? How can you celebrate your femininity?

_____

_____

_____

9. What is true or false about modesty? (write T or F and discuss with your Mom)

☐ being humble and not bragging about yourself
☐ showing off your developing body
☐ wearing short or tight clothes
☐ dressing with dignity so you are covered properly
☐ making sure that people notice your body parts first
☐ letting people first see your face and personality without distractions

10. What do you think it means to "dress with dignity"?

_____

_____

_____

11. Why is modesty important to your purity? Why is it important to God?

12. Discuss your emotional strengths and weaknesses with your Mom:

   - What makes you happy?
   - What makes you sad?
   - What makes you angry?
   - What makes you irritated?
   - What makes you nervous?
   - What other strong feelings do you have?
   - How are you doing so far managing your emotions?
   - How do you express your happy feelings of excitement, success, or anticipation?
   - How do you react so far to your negative feelings?
   - Can you be peaceful and calm when necessary? Are you often anxious? What are some ways to manage that? Ask your Mom for some ideas about it.

Chapter Reflections

While discussing this chapter, my Mom gave me some extra advice about . . .

While reading this chapter, I learned these two important things:

1. _____

2. _____

I resolve to live out the *LoveEd* teachings from this chapter by . . .

_____

_____

_____

End this chapter with the following prayer:

Dear God, my Creator, You have made me in amazing ways. When I study the science of life, I can't imagine what a genius You are. How did You get my food to digest, my heart to beat, and my lungs to breathe? And there is even more I don't know yet. Thank You for creating me. If I haven't yet told You that I appreciate You, I am telling You now: God, You are amazing! Amen.

My Mom and I completed this chapter on

_____

(date and time)

CHAPTER 5

Step by Step to a Life of Shining Love

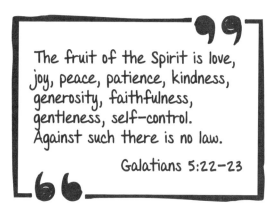

The fruit of the Spirit is love, joy, peace, patience, kindness, generosity, faithfulness, gentleness, self-control. Against such there is no law.

Galatians 5:22-23

A Diamond in the Rough

Have you ever seen a diamond? It is a clear, bright gem that glitters with light and beauty, and it is prized for its purity and durability. The word *diamond* comes from the Greek language and means "unbreakable." Diamonds are one of the hardest substances known to man and one of the most popular jewels for wedding rings. It takes billions of years for a diamond to form in the intense heat beneath the surface of the earth.

During puberty, think of yourself as a "diamond in the rough." This is an expression that describes a person who is still being polished, smoothed, or refined. You are a diamond in the rough because right now you may feel ordinary, but you have exceptional potential and a glorious future. God is shaping you into something even more precious and beautiful than you are right now. Just like a rugged little rock becomes a shiny diamond, you are being fashioned from a little girl into a woman who is pure and has a relationship with God that is unbreakable. Just like a diamond is so clear that it reflects all spectrums of light and color, our hearts can be so "clear" that we are filled with the light of God: "Blessed are the clean of heart, for they will see God" (Mt 5:8).

You are at the beginning of a new and exciting journey—growing from a girl into a woman—a journey where you will continue to discover the world and your mission in it. God created you for love. And as you walk the path of life, God wants you to *learn* to love and to *choose* to love.

Getting to the destination would be easy if the path were clear, wide, and smooth. But the path of life includes challenges and temptations. A successful journey starts with being smart, and that means being able to see the path ahead. You don't want to venture into new territory without a clear sense of direction. You need to get familiar with the landscape. You need to know where each path leads, where the dangers are, and how to make it safely to your destination.

This is a journey toward love, so being smart means knowing what real love is. Love is caring for other people, not just for yourself. It means being kind to your friends, respectful toward adults, and obedient to God. Love is sacrificing yourself for the good of others. Learning how to love your family and friends now will help you practice for your future as an adult.

Celebrate Being Strong

At the beginning of this book, we discussed what it means to be strong. We learned that strength is the ability to overcome temptations and make right choices for your body and soul. Your soul includes your mind, will, and emotions. God wants you to be strong in developing your talents. He wants you to treat your body in ways that are healthy and holy, such as eating right, exercising, and getting enough sleep. Whether or not your arms can lift hundred-pound weights or your legs can run a 10K race, your soul can learn to lift emotional burdens to God in prayer, and your heart can run after God. You can be strong in performing acts of kindness toward others.

Celebrate Being Smart

We also discussed the importance of being smart. The Bible calls this being "wise." Through wisdom, you learn to handle life in the real world. Wisdom not only applies to knowledge about the everyday circumstances of life but also to the bigger moral issues you will face. Through wisdom, you learn to make right decisions and know the difference between truth and lies. Wisdom helps you understand God's will.

When you go through temptations, trials, or difficulties, make a list of some "What Would Jesus Do?" answers. You will find that God *always* has an answer to every challenge, and you can trust Him to show you those answers in His own time.

The Goal Is Purity

To be pure means doing your best to follow God's rule of love. To do that, you need to have a relationship with God that is as unbreakable as a diamond. Even though you won't live life perfectly, and you will sometimes sin, you still need to strive to be pure. Did you forget to take out the trash after your mom asked you to? Did you yell at your brother? Did you think unkind thoughts about your best friend? When you make a wrong choice or commit a sin, don't let fear or shame keep you away from God's love! He has given us the most amazing way of being restored to fellowship with Him. It is called confession, or the Sacrament of Reconciliation. Confessing your sins to the priest during confession is one of the best ways to follow God's rule of love. Your soul will be washed clean again—and made pure!

Being pure also means keeping the junk out of your life. Have you ever seen a beautiful stream flowing with cold water that is so clear you can actually see the reflection of the sky? What happens if people start throwing trash into the stream? After a while, the perfect water becomes contaminated with old tires, soda bottles, and car batteries. The fish die, and the stream turns brown and begins to smell. The pure waters are now polluted.

Like this, your soul can become polluted. Our culture bombards us with "junk" through impure movies, music, magazines, TV, and websites. While entertainment and the Internet can be wonderful channels for learning and education, they can also be channels for spiritual pollution that lead to impurity. Advertisers try to get your attention through sexy images of immodestly dressed people. Be aware that TV shows, music, and the news applaud and promote twisted versions of friendships or marriages.

Being pure means replacing all the junk the culture throws our way with all the goodness God teaches us through the Church. Our world is filled with sexual images that try to destroy God's beautiful plan for boys and girls and men and women. When we see or hear impure words, sounds, or images on TV, the Internet, radio, or anywhere else, we need to be ready to turn away from them. Remember the steps for "being smart emotionally" in chapter 4? Follow the same steps when your eyes and ears are being bombarded by impurity:

1. Think: Acknowledge that this is a temptation that God wants you to resist.
2. Pray: "God, please give me the strength to run away from this temptation!"
3. Act: Turn off the computer, the TV, or the radio. Walk away from the images or people that are tempting you.

With God, all things are possible. He can help you develop self-control and courage. You have the power of the Holy Spirit living within you. Through His power, you can resist impure temptations. You can refuse to think, speak, listen to, watch, or look at the twisted version of love that destroys the beauty of God's plan for married love.

Modesty and Chastity Protect Your Purity

This is worth repeating: It's extremely important to develop the virtues of modesty and chastity. We spoke of modesty in the last chapter and the importance of dressing and talking with dignity. By choosing to wear cute yet modest clothing, you show that you are proud to be a young woman who deserves respect. By expressing chastity and self-control in your relationships with boys, you show that you are a friend instead of a flirt.

Chastity is the spiritual energy that directs your womanhood toward God's understanding of marriage rather than toward the selfish pleasure of using others and being used yourself. Chastity helps you transform your physical attractions to boys into a real and pure kind of friendship love. Through the virtue of chastity, you learn to manage your behavior and control your feelings. You learn to develop the kind of love that respects others and honors God, preparing you to become a loving adult someday.

Here are a few "Rules for the Road" on the journey to real love:

- Listen to music that speaks of beauty and love, not lust or using people.
- Use clean language and speak only to a trusted adult about private things.
- Choose *not* to watch impure shows that offend God's plan for love and life.
- Never let a phone or computer be a source of sin; block anything indecent.
- Take control of what you allow in your mind so you can fill it with goodness.
- Having a pure heart will let you see clearly the goodness and virtue of other people, especially the

attractive young men you will meet along the path of life.

Building a Strong Foundation for Love

Being pure and following God's "rule of love" begins with building a strong foundation for your soul. Rather than building with bricks and mortar or stones and cement, you are building the foundation of your life with God's truths. You receive these truths by listening to God, who speaks in many ways but mainly through His Church and the Scriptures.

How do you hear the words of Jesus? By listening to the priest who gives the homily during Mass or to your youth leader when he or she is teaching. Jesus speaks through the pope, the bishops, and your pastor. Jesus also speaks through your parents. In reality, God speaks through *every* circumstance of your life. Listening to His "words of life" and acting on them is like building a strong house on the rock. So listen to God's Word, and then, like Mary suggests, do whatever He tells you (see Jn 2:5). It isn't enough just to listen—you must also choose to follow Him.

Now that you are building the foundation of your soul (mind, will, and emotions) to be strong, smart, and pure, you may be wondering: What's the next step? Unlike a house that requires wood or stone, your soul requires virtues to build on the foundation of God's truth. A virtue gives you spiritual energy that boosts your power to share God's love. The opposite of choosing to live by virtues is to choose vices, which are evil. Vices include dishonesty, meanness, disobedience, impurity, and laziness. The virtues to fight those vices are honesty, kindness, obedience, faithfulness, and perseverance.

Light for Your Soul

A pure heart is like that diamond that reflects all spectrums of light. When we have pure hearts and pure souls, we are able to see the path ahead of us more clearly. In God's light, we see the right choices that were not obvious in the darkness. Being pure isn't easy though. To be pure during puberty—and beyond—requires practice. Following God's "rule of love" becomes easier when you exercise good habits by making one good choice at a time. Let's join Mariana again to see how she and her friends are growing in virtue.

Mariana was hosting her second annual autumn slumber party. This year, Sarah decided not to come, but that was okay because Mariana was starting to spend more time with her friends Rosie and Francine, and she also invited Becky and Natalia again.

"That's hilarious, Mariana," Francine said, as she watched Mariana do circus acrobat tricks with her little sister, Bella. "Let me show you the exercise I do with my little brother."

Francine laid down on the floor and put her feet up in the air. She carefully lifted Bella up onto her feet and suspended her there like a flying airplane. Bella laughed as she flung her arms out in front of her.

"Me-be-super-girl," Bella tried to say. All the girls laughed.

Mrs. Garcia came in the room. "You girls are certainly noisy, but it sounds like a happy noise! It's great to hear you laughing. Sorry to break up the fun here, but it's time for

Bella to go to bed. You girls can stay up for another hour though—just keep it a little more quiet."

"Okay, Mom," promised Mariana.

"We will, too, Mrs. Garcia," said Francine, Rosie, Natalia, and Becky in unison.

Mariana felt comfortable with her friends, and she was especially happy that they were willing to be obedient to her mom.

"Thanks, everyone, for respecting my mom. I want you to know how happy I am to have friends who want to be good, too. It's not always easy to obey and be good, but when I know my friends are trying, it helps me to be better, too."

"My mom said that obedience pleases God when you obey right away and without complaining," said Francine. "It's so hard to practice that when she asks me to take out the smelly garbage or do the dishes, but I'm working on it."

Rosie chimed in next. "My big sister tells me that if I don't obey my parents now, I'll never be able to follow the rules of the road and learn to drive a car or be able to keep a job when I grow up."

"I was wondering if this obedience now would pay off later," said Natalia, laughing, "but I guess we'll have to take your sister's word for it."

"I've read lots of stories this year about how obedience pays off," said Becky. "Our religious ed teacher gave us a whole lesson on obedience. She had some of us act out the story of Noah, and others the story of Abraham. I don't know if I am as obedient to God yet as Abraham was, but I'm going to keep practicing."

"One good choice at a time," proclaimed Mariana, "That's what my mom always says."

"Hey, remember at last year's slumber party when we

prayed for my sister because she stopped going to church?" Rosie asked. "Well, guess what, this year her new college roommate is very active in the church there on campus, and she invited my sister to go with her on a retreat. Now my sister is going to church again!"

"Do you think it was God answering our prayers that made her come back?" Becky questioned.

"I bet it was," declared Mariana. "God has answered lots of my prayers, even though they are just little things, like helping me study for a test or run faster in the track meet."

Natalia was quiet. "My mom still isn't going to church yet, so we need to pray for her again this year. Maybe we all should pray for her more often. I love my mom so much, and I want her to go to Mass with us again so badly that sometimes I feel like crying."

"Let's pray a decade of the Rosary for her right now," suggested Rosie. "And maybe by next year . . ."

All the girls smiled in agreement, and Mariana went down to the family room to grab some rosaries out of their family bowl of extra ones. Mrs. Garcia had just finished putting Bella to sleep and was downstairs saying her night prayers.

"What do you need, Mariana?" Mrs. Garcia asked.

"Oh, my friends and I are going to pray the Rosary, Mom, so I'm getting our extras."

Mrs. Garcia just smiled and continued to pray, adding a prayer of gratitude to God for Mariana and her friends and the fun they were having just being together.

After their prayer, the girls chatted a bit more about the challenges of being good and growing in virtue. Becky wanted to talk about her situation. "My parents are still separated, and I know how sad it is for my family, even though mom says it is the best thing. If I ever get married, I want to figure out a way to have a marriage that never breaks up."

"C'mon, Becky, we are only eleven years old—how can we know that now?" asked Natalia.

"My family counselor told all of us kids that we can practice faithfulness now in everything we do to help us be faithful in the future. He said we could be strong and smart about all our decisions so we can have a faithful marriage later. He said we should have hope and trust in God and always let Him lead when we make a decision about dating or marriage."

"My mom said that marriage is about the virtue of perseverance," said Rosie. "My parents don't always see things the same way, but I know that neither of them will ever give up."

Mariana nodded and agreed. "I have a lot of work to do on that virtue, too, before I get older. I can barely practice my piano lessons each day, let alone remember my night prayers. I get tired and discouraged easily. Maybe you all can pray for me on that one," she said with a laugh.

"Hey, as long as we're praying for each other, let's pray for honesty," said Natalia. "My brother has lost my parents' trust because he is sneaking around behind their backs, exaggerating about stuff, and sometimes even lying. I pray that I can be stronger than that when it comes to being honest, but sometimes I have a hard time with it, too."

"Hey, this is not confession, people!" yelled Becky so loudly that the girls realized they could be heard outside the room.

They all started laughing and giggling. "I have an idea," said Mariana. "Let's all be best friends forever—the type of friends that help each other be good. Let's always be friends who are kind to each other and everyone else. Let's be faithful, let's be honest, and please, since my mom is on this 'dress modestly' campaign, let's all wear clothes that are modest, too. Then we can make modesty the trend. My mom said that if you hang out with friends who have your family values, you will grow stronger on the inside."

"Okay, I'm in," said Becky.

"So am I," agreed Natalia.

"Me, too," declared Rosie, "and if any of you ever decide to stop going to church like my sister did, I'm not going to sit by and watch. I am coming over to your house on Sunday morning and tossing a bucketful of ice water on your head until you get up and come to church with me."

The girls all roared in laughter. "Friends forever!" they chanted.

Mrs. Garcia heard them laughing. "Girls, it's time to go to sleep now."

"Yes, Mom!" they all cheered together, and after one more set of giggles, Mariana turned off all the lights except the small night-light shining on five happy faces.

Wrap It Up

God has given you the mission of sharing His love with the world. Right now, your "world" may be your school or your neighborhood. When you grow up, your world will expand to include your entire community and local parish. No matter how big your world becomes, or how far you travel, you will always be in the center of the circle of God's love. When you turn to Him, listen to Him, obey Him, and pray to Him, you will receive all of the blessings and grace you need. In the circle of God's love you will grow into a strong, smart, and pure young woman!

There's a lot to learn as you prepare for the journey. But here's the most important thing to remember: God loves you and will walk with you every step of the way. God is your ultimate guide. And He has so much to give you to help you on your journey.

During this journey of puberty, you will be traveling between the two circles of family and friends. Every circle is kept within the one enormous circle of God's love. Being aware of His love and learning how to share that love with others will bring you joy. Your joy will be more brilliant than the shining light of that beautiful diamond, leading the way to Christ!

God wants you to be smart. He has given you an intellect so you can understand His plan for life and love. And He gives you His wisdom through the Church, the Bible, the saints, your parents, and your teachers.

God wants you to be strong. He has given you freewill so you can make good choices, especially about love and purity. He gives you the virtue of chastity and the Sacraments of Holy Communion and Reconciliation to keep your soul strong.

Finally, God wants you to be pure. He gives you a desire for true love and deep, lasting relationships. When your heart is pure, you can clearly see the purpose of your life: to become the loving person God created you to be.

Decide now to be strong, smart, and pure on your journey to love!

Discussion Questions

Answer and discuss these questions with your Mom.

1. What does it mean to be strong on the inside?

_____

_____

_____

2. What does it mean to be smart?

_____

_____

_____

3. What are some ways you can keep your mind pure?

_____

_____

_____

4. What can you do now to build spiritual strengths such as:

Faithfulness:

Honesty:

Obedience:

Self-control:

Chapter Reflections

While discussing this chapter, my Mom gave me some extra advice about . . .

_____

_____

_____

While reading this chapter, I learned these two important things:

1. _____

2. _____

I resolve to live out the _LoveEd_ teachings from this chapter by . . .

_____

_____

_____

End this chapter with the following prayer:

Holy Spirit, fill my heart with all the good that you want me to have. After all, You are love! Guide me on this journey of becoming a loving person. Speak to my heart in those little whispers each day when I need to be patient or kind. Send me the people I need in my life that can help me be strong and faithful. Amen.

My Mom and I completed this chapter on

_____

(date and time)

CHAPTER 6

The Gift of Myself Back to God

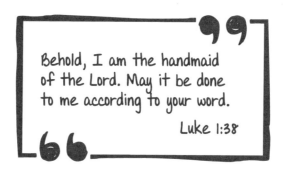

Behold, I am the handmaid of the Lord. May it be done to me according to your word.

Luke 1:38

You are now ready for the grand adventure of beginning to be a strong, smart, and pure young woman as you grow up. If you will follow the ideas and suggestions in this book, you can become a virtuous young woman who has much to give back to God. As a Catholic, you will always have a reason to celebrate life, love, and happiness.

Throughout this book, we have shared escapades, troubles, and joys with our friend, Mariana. She has been learning, too, how to be strong, smart, and pure. She has been discovering the gift of her femininity, which blossoms during this time of physical change called puberty. She is learning to discover her talents and areas of interest, which are uniquely hers and which she will use as she decides what to do with her life. She is learning to make new friends who will be with her on the journey. Most importantly, Mariana has been discovering the three circles of love—and her special and unique place in the middle of them all.

In the center of the family circle, Mariana has been learning how to receive and give love. Her friendship circle is helping her grow in the virtues of faithfulness and kindness as she learns to be a good friend to others and choose good friends for herself. The romance circle is the place she will one day meet a young man and get married, if she chooses. With God's love as the enormous circle holding together the other three, Mariana—and *you*—can freely learn how to live and grow into strong, smart, and pure young ladies during puberty and beyond.

During puberty, you will change physically, mentally, emotionally, and spiritually. As you put into practice the lessons you've learned in this book, you will find that puberty is a glorious adventure, full of challenges and surprises. Trust God to guide you through it all, and celebrate your place in the center of His love! Rely on the goodness of your family, friends, and church, and you, too, will be able to say along with Mariana, "I am becoming a strong, smart, and pure young lady!"

A Moment with Mariana

The bright light filtered through the drapes in the living room. Mariana opened her eyes. Her friends were still asleep in their sleeping bags. Quietly she got up and went into the kitchen where her father was preparing two cups of coffee.

"Good morning, Punkin'!" he said, giving her a kiss on the cheek. "Did you have a fun slumber party?"

Mariana nodded and yawned. "Yes, it's been great."

After hearing her friends' prayer requests the night before, Mariana had a burning question in her heart. "Dad, can I ask you something?"

"Sure, honey," said her father, sitting down at the table with his coffee. "Make it quick—I need to take this coffee upstairs to your mom! She had a rough night with your little sister."

Mariana frowned. She knew her mother must be very tired after staying up with a cranky, teething baby.

"Okay, well, this is what I wanted to know. What makes you and mom stay together? What makes you stay with the Church?"

Her father smiled. "Those are big questions," he answered.

Mariana sighed. "Well," she explained, "One of my friend's parents are separated, and someone else's mom stopped going to church."

Her father's expression became serious as he set his coffee mug on the table. "You know, some people struggle with their marriages. Some people struggle with the Church. We all struggle. But everyone has been given a choice. It's the people who choose to open their hearts to God's plan for love that end up making the right choices. God's love helps your mom and I stay together! His love teaches us to be unselfish and forgive each other. His love helps us go to Mass because that's where we hear God's words and receive the gift of Holy Communion."

Her father stood up and took the mugs of coffee into his big, strong hands. "Now," he said, "I need to take this coffee to your mom—she deserves a little break!"

Her father briskly walked toward the staircase with the coffee. Watching his tall figure walk away, Mariana felt a warm happiness well up in her heart. She felt strong enough to jump over a building! The love of her father toward her mother was showing her the pathway to God. She knew that God was a good heavenly Father, who gave good gifts to His children. She knew because her own father consistently showed her mother, her sisters, and her unconditional love.

Mariana leaned against the kitchen sink. Looking out the kitchen window at the rising sun that gleamed on the autumn trees, Mariana saw Sarah's house out the window and thought about her friend. She wished Sarah could have been there last night to laugh and pray with them. Over a year ago, she had invited Sarah to her birthday party. Even though Sarah had not been a very good friend to her, Mariana had mustered the courage to invite Sarah because of something Mariana's mother had told her: "Real friends never give up on each other."

Still watching the sunrise, Mariana thought about her mother's words. She remembered how, with determination, she had reached down and grabbed the crumpled invitation she had thrown on the floor. She remembered smoothing out the invitation as she began writing, "Sarah, you are invited to my Eleventh Birthday Party!" Mariana remembered the day she delivered the invitation to Sarah. It was a beautiful moment of tears and forgiveness. They had hugged each other and promised to spend more time together.

Even though Sarah went to a different school and still made some wrong choices about friends and TV shows, Mariana still loved her, missed her, and tried to share the love of God with her. She couldn't forget that she and Sarah had once shared many wonderful times together, from

Fourth of July celebrations to silly moments of hilarious laughter while eating cookies at the kitchen table. *"Yes,"* thought Mariana, as she watched the golden-pink sky grow brighter outside the window, *"mom is right. Real friends never give up on each other."*

But Mariana felt more comfortable with her new friends now than she did with Sarah. She felt safe and supported with Becky, Natalia, Rosie, and Francine. They could laugh together and pray together. No one tempted anyone to watch bad movies or go online. They just talked and had fun. "Maybe, just maybe," Mariana thought, "Sarah will join us again. She could laugh with us and make fun food with us. She could have fun again like we used to. Well . . . maybe someday."

Though it was still early in the morning, Mariana felt like doing something nice for her friends who were still sleeping in the other room. She decided to make breakfast for everyone. As Mariana scrubbed her hands at the kitchen sink, she remembered another important moment. She recalled the time just before she had started sixth grade. From upstairs in her bedroom, she remembered hearing her father call, "Mariana, your mother and I want to talk to you." Sitting down on the living room couch, Mariana remembered how her parents had lovingly talked with her about the autumn dance in September. Wisely, her parents had told her that she needed to be older and more mature before she began a romantic relationship with a boy. After an hour of reading, prayer, and more discussion, Mariana had seen the wisdom of her parents. She was glad to enjoy middle school by being friends with everyone.

Mariana had learned a lot from her mom and dad. Her father had explained that friendship love is not the same as romantic love. "Friends," he had said, "grow together spiritually by doing good things together and by working together to feed the poor or help the sick. Friends also learn about themselves and others through hobbies, or talents, or special activities."

Mariana liked the way her father had described friendship. She liked the fact that together they had decided she would hold a sleepover party with a few close friends on the night of the dance. This was now the second year for having a sleepover instead of going to the dance. As usual, her mother had helped her make special snacks, and her mom had taken the girls roller-skating before dinner.

Thinking back to her year in sixth grade, Mariana smiled. She was so happy her parents had helped her make the right decision about the autumn dance. Turning toward the fridge, Mariana pulled out a carton of eggs, some bread, and some milk. Pulling a few pans and bowls from the shelves, Mariana began preparing breakfast.

Mariana began dipping the thick slices of bread into the French toast batter. The sun was rising higher now, and yet she could hear her friends still snoring in the other room. Mariana yawned, feeling tired. She would have liked to snuggle in her sleeping bag and get some more sleep. But the example her father had set for her made her keep going. He was taking a nice, hot cup of coffee to his very tired wife. She was glad her parents did nice things for each other.

Mariana thought about what she had learned in her youth group at church about families and marriage. Her youth group leader, Sam, had told them that it takes two—one man and one woman—to create a family.

Sam said, "God's ideal plan is that all children everywhere grow up in the center of the circle of family, with their original mom and dad. God's plan is that each child learns to receive and give love in the family circle, with a married man and woman at the very center. This doesn't always happen, though, because some families are separated by divorce." Mariana remembered feeling very surprised when her youth leader talked about divorce and how it hurt moms, dads, and kids.

As Mariana sprinkled cinnamon in the batter, she thought about how Becky had talked about her family, asking everyone to pray for her mom and dad who were now separated. The other girls had gathered around her and hugged her. After they had all prayed together, Mariana shared some wise words with Becky that she had learned from their youth minister.

"Have hope, Becky! Hope is a virtue that we can practice with the help of God. Hope helps us stay focused and happy, even when bad things are happening all around us."

Becky nodded and sniffled. "I hope my parents will get back together."

"We'll keep praying," Mariana had answered.

Mariana whisked the eggs in a bowl and wondered, *"What does it mean to be strong?"* Just then, her father appeared from around the corner, carrying her baby sister, Bella, who was nestled against his chest and half asleep.

"Well, I see my daughter is making breakfast! Wonderful!" Mariana continued whipping the eggs together into a frothy liquid so she could scramble them later.

"Dad, what does it mean to be strong, smart, and pure?"

Her father looked off in the distance and rocked Bella in his arms. "Well, strength is more than having big muscles or fast legs. Strength is the ability to make the right choices for your body and soul. Your soul includes your mind, will, and emotions. When you choose to do good and healthy actions that please God, you are being strong! When you make good choices for your body and soul, you bring glory to God!"

Mariana thought for a moment. "Having a slumber party instead of going to the dance was a good choice, right?"

"Yes," her father replied. "You made a good choice. You showed that you're strong. You're also becoming smarter all the time."

"Oh, Dad," Mariana said, "I'm not all that smart! I got a C in math this semester, remember?"

Her father laughed. "But you tried your best, right?"

Mariana nodded as she poured the eggs into a hot frying pan. Her father continued, "Through God's gift of wisdom you learn how to handle life in the real world. Right now, you're learning how to take out the garbage and keep your room organized so you can find your clothes and books in the morning before school."

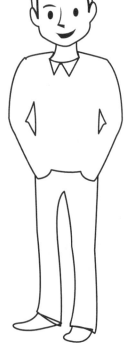

Mariana laughed. "Yes, Dad, I know I'm a slob! But I'm trying to keep my stuff organized better."

Her father nodded, patting Bella gently on the back as he rocked her back and forth. "Yes, you are! And later, you may learn to do new things, like managing your allowance money or changing the oil in your car. But wisdom is not only

about the everyday circumstances of life; it's for the bigger moral issues you'll face."

Getting out the butter and jam from the fridge, Mariana sighed. "I guess I'm learning how to be strong and smart. But I'm still not sure about what it means to be pure."

Her father smiled and put the pacifier in Bella's mouth while Mariana continued to gather items for the breakfast. Just then, Mariana's mother walked into the room. "Well, here are some of my favorite people! Making breakfast, no less!" she said.

Mr. Garcia leaned over and kissed his wife on the cheek. "You're just in time to answer Mariana's question. She wants to know what it means to be pure."

Mariana's mother walked over to the stove and stirred the eggs as Mariana began pulling glasses and plates from the cabinet.

"Well," she began, "to be pure means doing our best to follow God's rule of love. To do that, we need to have a relationship with God that is as unbreakable as . . . ," her voice trailed off. She suddenly looked down at her hand and smiled. "It needs to be as clear and unbreakable as this diamond in my wedding ring!" she said triumphantly. Her ring glittered in the clear morning light.

"That's right," agreed Mariana's father. "God wants us to have a strong relationship with Him, and a diamond ring is a perfect example because diamonds are so strong they can't be broken!"

Her parents smiled at one another. "Even though we won't be perfect, and we sometimes sin, we still need to strive to be pure in our love for God and others," Mariana's mother explained. "Your purity starts now as you focus on God's will and try not to grow up too fast. Having a slumber party instead of going to the dance is part of that. As you enter your teens, you can make a choice to be faithful to your future husband, even before you ever meet him. Just keep being obedient to God's plan for love."

Mariana's father continued rocking the sleeping baby as Mariana and her mother finished the breakfast preparations. Inside, Mariana felt warm and cozy. She felt safe in the circle of family and happy to be her parent's daughter. She felt happy with her friends and what they talked about at the slumber party. She was learning how to receive and give love. She was learning how to be unselfish by serving others. She was becoming a good friend to others and earning their love in the circle of friendship. With the help of family and friends—and especially God—Mariana knew that she truly was growing strong, smart, and pure.

From the other room, she heard her friends stirring. Mariana couldn't wait to share breakfast with them. It was her way of helping her friends feel the love of God, even in the middle of their troubles. It was her way of giving herself to others. She was a gift to them, and they were a gift to her. It was her way of showing love to her mom, dad, older sister, and even sometimes her cranky baby sister.

"Come and get it!" she called. "Breakfast is ready!"

Final Meditation

How do Catholics meditate?

As you get older, you'll want your prayers to become more mature, too. You've probably learned many verbal prayers so far, and that's good. You should continue to say these verbal prayers for the rest of your life. The *Catechism* teaches us that the next level of prayer is part of a quest to understand the why and how of the Christian life. To do this, you can pay close attention to what God is saying to you in order for you to know and do His will. You can sit and think about one of the Gospel stories and imagine yourself learning from Jesus while He was on earth, or you can ponder a sunny sky and think about His ascension into heaven, or you can concentrate on any lesson from God you can learn better. Most importantly, you try to apply it to your own life. Here is a way to start:

Early in the morning, before you launch into your day, find a quiet place and put yourself in God's presence. He is everywhere; He encompasses all the other circles you are a part of. He's with you now. Ask Him to help you be aware of His presence, now and always. Talk to God about all the changes that are happening in your life. He knows all about the changes in your body—it's all unfolding according to His plan. Thank God for helping you to show His love to the world in your own unique way.

Thank Him for your friends by name. Ask for His help to be a good friend and always lead them closer to Him. Thank Him for the good times you have and ask forgiveness for any times you have failed to have their best interests at heart; for any bad examples you have given, or for any times you may have led them into sin. Ask for God's strength to be a good example so you can help your friends to be smart, strong, and pure, too.

Thank God for creating men and women. Thank Him that you are a young woman now and for all the natural talents and strengths He's blessed you with. Thank Him for the boys in your life, for all you can learn from and admire in them. Ask Him for the grace to be a good friend to those boys, to respect them, and help them grow into strong, healthy men.

Ask God for guidance as you grow older and begin to have romantic feelings. And turn often to Mary, who is the purest example of womanhood and available to help you grow in virtue.

Talk to God about your vocation. If you think there's a possibility you might have a calling to religious or consecrated life, thank God for that thought. Ask for His help to stay pure if He's preparing you for a life of celibacy and service to others.

If you feel called to marriage, thank God for that thought. Ask for God's help to stay pure in preparation for giving yourself totally to your future husband. Pray for him—he's out there! Ask God to help you find him when the time is right.

Lift up your heart toward God and tell Him you want to follow His plan. Tell Him you're willing to embrace all the sacrifice required to live up to His calling for you.

Before you end your prayer time, ask God to show you one practical way you can follow His plan of love better— something practical you can do. Ask God to remind you of this throughout the day. Maybe write it down in your journal or on an index card. You can review it tonight when you examine your conscience.

End your meditation by slowly praying an Our Father, a Hail Mary, and a Glory Be, offering your day to God in a sincere gift of yourself.

A Reflection for Your Mom

Give the book to your Mom so she can take time to reflect on her own.

Take some time in the morning to put yourself in God's presence before the rush of the day. Ask Him to help you become aware of His presence so you can live each day knowing He is always with you.

Maybe it's been a while since you took some time for reflection. Thank God for the opportunity to grow closer to Him. You have an amazing project in common: this incredible daughter He has given you. God has entrusted this precious soul to you so that you can lead her along the pathways of His plan. By following this program you have renewed your own knowledge of God's plan.

Thank God for your own parents and for their sacrifice and dedication. Forgive them from your heart if there were shortcomings or issues in your relationship. If they have passed away, commend their souls to God. If they are still alive, thank God for their continuing help in your life.

Thank God for your husband and his love for you. Thank Him for the vocation of marriage. Ask God to strengthen your marriage so it can show God's love to the world through your mutual self-giving. Even though romantic feelings come and go, ask God for the resolve to be a support to your husband always. If you're experiencing any marital problems, ask God's forgiveness for your part in them and promise you will do all in your power, with His grace, to overcome them. Ask for the grace to put your family first–before your career, before any selfish interests, before everything. Thank God for your vocation as a wife and mother.

Thank God for your children, especially for this wondrous girl with whom you are reading this book. Think about all the God-given goodness in her, all her talents. Ask forgiveness for those times you may have neglected her or put other concerns before her. Promise God to be as steadfast with her as the Virgin Mary was for Jesus, teaching her what is true, good, and beautiful.

Ask for forgiveness if you have had any faults against purity. Promise God that you will strive to make your house a haven of virtue and goodness. Ask for God's help to serve your family with grace and generosity. Thank God for entrusting you with your family. Seek God's grace and protection as you help your family to heaven.

Make a commitment before God to be the kind of wife your husband needs and the kind of mother your daughter needs to become the woman God intends her to be.

Before you end your prayer time, ask God to show you one tangible way you can follow God's plan of love better—something practical you can do. Ask God to remind you of this throughout the day. Maybe write it down in your journal or on an index card. You can review it tonight when you examine your conscience.

End by praying slowly an Our Father, a Hail Mary, and a Glory Be, offering your day to God in a sincere gift of yourself.

Mom and daughter, read together Luke 2:41-52 about Jesus when He was twelve years old. Discuss why it is important to always obey God the Father in order to grow in wisdom and in grace.

Mom, now give your daughter a big hug. Tell her how much you love her and make a promise together to dedicate yourselves to being strong, smart, and pure.

Notes

Notes

Notes

Notes